Simple and Practical
Taxation

A Guide to PAYE, National Insurance, VAT and Schedule D Income Tax

Keith Kirkland and Stuart Howard

**KOGAN
PAGE**

YOURS TO HAVE AND TO HOLD
BUT NOT TO COPY

First published in 1998

Kogan Page Limited
120 Pentonville Road
London N1 9JN

Vector Business Development
Vector House, Titchfield
Hants PO15 6RR

© Vector Business Development, 1998

Illustrations by John Loader

British Library Cataloguing in Publication Data

A CIP record for this book is available from the British Library

ISBN 0 7494 2941 0

Typeset by Vector Business Development.
Printed and bound in Great Britain by Bell & Bain Ltd, Glasgow.

Contents

Chapter 1

Introduction

There are many forms of taxation. In this book, we look at five taxes of particular interest to smaller businesses. These are:

1   Income Tax under Schedule 'D' (tax on self employed profits)

2   Value Added Tax

3   National Insurance

4   Income Tax under Schedule 'E' (PAYE)

5   Corporation Tax

This book will introduce taxation to you, but it will not make you a tax expert. Take proper advice before making any tax decisions. If you read this book, you should be able to discuss tax matters in greater depth with your adviser.

Treat practical exercises in this workbook as examples only. Before making calculations for yourself, check that you are using the current tax rates and allowances.

Although every care has been taken to ensure that the text is correct, be careful as tax legislation is full of obscure exceptions and limitations. Not all of these limitations have been reproduced in this workbook (since it would make the text totally indigestible). Check the detail with one of the tax publications listed in Appendix 1.

We hope this book will prove useful. As Benjamin Franklin said: *'In life nothing is more certain than death and taxes.'*

Chapter 2

Income Tax – Schedule D

Who Pays Schedule D Income Tax?

Persons are taxed under Schedule D if they operate as a sole trader or partnership. These are defined below.

Sole Trader

A sole trader is an individual who owns and operates a business. 'Sole', in this context, refers to the business ownership since sole traders can have as many employees as they choose.

Sole Trader

Partnership

A partnership is the relationship which exists between two or more people operating a business with a view to making profits. You do not need a written agreement to constitute a partnership – merely acting together is evidence enough.

However, common sense dictates that anyone entering into a serious business relationship like partnership ought to have a written partnership agreement. Partners are 'jointly and severally' liable for business debt. This means that partnership debts are the responsibility of all the partners, any of whom can be sued for non-payment. A partnership can have any number of employees.

Partnership

In theory, sole traders and partnerships could grow to become very large businesses. In practice, once the business reaches a certain size, most owners convert the business to a limited liability company. Companies, by the way, pay corporation tax not income tax.

What is Schedule D?

Schedule D is one form of income tax. There used to be six schedules (or sources) of income tax. However, Schedule B was abolished in 1988 leaving five schedules currently in use. These are:

Schedule A	Rents for land and unfurnished lettings
Schedule C	Certain interest taxed at source
Schedule D	Profits from trade and certain investment income
Schedule E	Income from employment
Schedule F	Dividends from companies.

Each schedule comprises a set of rules which define the types of income caught within that category. The schedule also dictates which kinds of expense are allowable for tax relief and which are not.

Schedule D is divided into six cases:

Case I	Profits from a trade or business
Case II	Profits from a profession or vocation
Case III	Interest *not* taxed at source (eg National Savings interest)
Case IV	Interest on securities outside the UK (eg foreign dividends)
Case V	Income from possessions outside the UK
Case VI	Income not included elsewhere.

Clearly, Cases I and II apply to the overwhelming majority of self employed people. These notes only relate to Cases I and II. In practice, the two are so similar that we can regard them as the same thing. Under the rules of Schedule D, every sole trader or partnership has to pay tax on the profits of the business.

These profits are normally calculated by an accountant using information provided by the business. However, there is nothing in law to prevent the owners calculating their own profits and agreeing their own tax liability. Indeed, self assessment was designed to make the calculation of Schedule D income tax easier. The self assessment form is submitted to the local tax inspector for approval, often accompanied by a copy of the profit and loss account and balance sheet. The tax inspector will check that the profit figure looks plausible. If the inspector is uncertain, he will ask the owner or his accountant to justify the calculations. Once the profit figure is accepted by the Inland Revenue then the tax liability can be computed.

In practice, you hardly ever pay tax on the exact profit figure shown in the accounts. You normally have to make adjustments for the following reasons:

- Some business expenses are not allowed as tax deductions. These include items such as entertaining and expensive gifts. Other costs are only allowed in part. For example, a car used in the business will normally be used part for business and part for pleasure. Only that part relating to business use attracts taxation relief (see page 9).

- Purchases of plant and equipment cannot be deducted as a lump sum in their year of acquisition. Instead, the relief is shared out over subsequent years. These reliefs are called capital allowances. Normally, you add back your own 'wear and tear' allowance called 'depreciation' and subtract the value of the capital allowance instead. Capital allowances are explained on page 7.

- Everyone is entitled to earn a certain slice of income free of all taxes. This is called their 'personal allowance'. Personal allowances are covered in more detail later in this chapter (see page 11).

Businesses with a turnover of £15,000 or less can elect to submit a simple three line account consisting of turnover, purchases and a note of the resulting net profit.

Tax payments can be payable many months after the profit was earned. Be sure to keep enough cash in reserve to meet the debt when it finally arrives!

Businesses pay tax in three instalments. These are explained later in this chapter.

Allowable Business Expenses

Expenses

In principle, it is easy to decide which items are tax deductible. A business expense which is 'wholly and exclusively' incurred for business purposes is allowable. Because of the wide nature of business, almost any expenditure could become an allowable expenditure for someone. The following list shows some typical allowable expenditures:

- Materials bought for resale.

- Wages and salaries (including temporary staff).

- Advertising and promotion.

- Hire of plant and equipment.

- Interest on business loans.

Hire charges are allowable

- Insurance, eg public liability, business profits etc.

- Repairs and maintenance for plant, equipment and property.

- VAT where the trader is not registered and is, therefore, unable to reclaim input tax.

- Administrative costs including business rates, rent, telephone, stationery, postage, heat, light.

- Professional fees for accounting or legal charges (but not tax appeals or personal tax advice).

- Travel on business trips at home and abroad. Also running costs of vehicles used for business purposes.

There is no magic list of expenses which are automatically tax allowable. Remember, almost any item of expenditure will be allowable for someone. The key question is this – 'Is this expense a true cost of operating the business?'. If the answer is 'No' then the expenditure is not tax allowable.

Note that you are not allowed to 'bend the rules' simply because you have similar expenditure at home and at work. For example, the cost of a painter and decorator is an allowable business expense when decorating your office. You cannot send the decorator to work at your home and claim the decorator's wages as a business expense. When working at your home, the decorator becomes a personal cost and is definitely not tax allowable.

Capital Allowances

Most businesses need to purchase some form of plant, equipment or vehicles. As time progresses, these items gradually wear out and lose value. This loss in value is shown in the accounts as 'depreciation'. Depreciation, however, is not allowable as a business expense. Any deductions shown in the accounts have to be added back when calculating taxable profits.

It would, however, be unfair not to allow the business some measure of relief to reflect capital expenditure. This is provided via capital allowances. The rules regarding capital allowances are complex and change frequently. It is advisable, therefore, to keep up to date. Capital allowances can be claimed on a wide variety of capital expenditure but, for our purposes, we will concentrate on the main group which is plant and machinery.

Plant and machinery comprise all items of fixed or movable equipment kept for permanent use in the business. It includes, for example, fixtures, fittings, plant and vehicles. Instead of keeping a detailed record of each item, the Inland Revenue allows for common items to be grouped together in 'pools'. Separate pools *must* be kept for:

- all motor cars costing less than £12,000
- each car costing more than £12,000
- each asset used partly for private use.

All other items can be collected together in one pool.

An annual allowance of 25% of the value of the pool is given and this is referred to as the 'writing down allowance' (WDA). The reduced value of the asset is then referred to as the 'written down value' (WDV), or 'the book value'.

Procedures can become complicated when an asset is sold. We will not consider this aspect today except to mention the following point for items in a *separate* pool. If the asset is sold for less than the written down value, a loss on disposal can be claimed – this is called a 'balancing allowance'. If the asset is sold for more than its written down value then you will be charged for a gain on disposal. This is called a 'balancing charge' which is added to profit and taxed.

Detailed examples of capital allowances are shown in Appendix 4 (see page 171).

Non Allowable Expenses

The following expenses are not allowed for business taxation purposes:

- Personal or domestic expenditure.

- Taking business stock for personal use.

- Personal drawings.

- Entertaining expenses (with the exception of a staff Christmas party – providing the cost does not exceed £75 per head)

- Payment of your personal income tax or capital gains tax.

Entertaining is not tax deductible

- Depreciation – remember, however, that the Inland Revenue substitute their form of 'standardised depreciation' called capital allowances instead.

- Fines for illegal acts and connected legal expenses.

- Political donations (except under very special circumstances).

Apportioned Expenses

Certain expenditure can be part business and part private. Examples include use of home as office, use of motor car, telephone etc. At first glance, this seems to fall foul of the Act's 'wholly and exclusively for business' test. In practice, common sense prevails and these costs are apportioned between private and business use.

For example, you may agree with the Inland Revenue that 60% of your mileage is business use and 40% is private use. In this case, 60% of the total costs of running the motor car will be allowed for taxation purposes. You may find it worthwhile keeping records of your mileage to support your claim.

Exercise 1   Would the following expenses qualify for tax relief?

		Yes	No	Partly
1	Travel home to work			
2	Equipment depreciation			
3	Interest on loan from relative			
4	Cost of guard dog			
5	Use of home telephone			
6	Owner's drawings			
7	Speeding fine			
8	Owner's car insurance			
9	Accountant's charges			
10	Entertaining foreign businessmen			
11	Owner's pension fund			

Check your answers with page 157.

The Tax Calculation So Far

An adjustment must be made to the accounting profit to reflect allowable and disallowable expenditure. The calculation could look like that shown below:

	£
Net profit per accounts	58000
Add back	
Depreciation	10000
Private use of car	2000
Private use of telephone	250
Adjusted profit	70250
Deduct	
Capital allowances	(11000)
Assessable profit	59250

Note: The net profit figure must not include any deductions for owners' personal drawings. We still need to take into account a further adjustment – 'personal allowances'. Personal allowances are explained next.

Personal Allowances

Every person is entitled to a slice of tax free income. This is called their personal allowance. The allowance normally varies from year to year. It is usually changed annually in the budget. There are several forms of allowance:

The Personal Allowance – everyone is entitled to this allowance. People over the ages of 65 and 75 have higher personal allowances than those below these ages (see page 39 for details). People over pension age whose income is more than £16,200 (1998/99) have £1 of personal allowance withdrawn for every £2 of income in excess of £16,200 until they reach the normal personal allowance for those below retirement age. For 1998/99 the personal allowance for those below retirement age is £4,195.

Married Couples Allowance – each couple has a married couples allowance. Married couples over the ages of 65 and 75 have higher allowances than those below these ages (see page 39 for details). The married couples allowance was treated more flexibly from 6 April 1993. Now it can go all to the husband, or all to the wife, or be split equally between them. An election must be made before the tax year if the allowance is to be given partly, or wholly, to the wife. For 1998/99 the married couples allowance for those below retirement age is £1,900. However, the tax relief for the allowance is restricted to 15%. We will see later how to apply this restriction in the tax calculation.

Additional Relief for Children – this is given to single parent families. The relief is set at the same level as the married couples allowance. For 1998/99 this is £1,900. Again, this allowance is restricted to 15%. The allowance is available providing the child is below the age of 16 or remains in full time education. Only one allowance is available regardless of how many children there are.

Widows Bereavement Allowance – this relief is also set at the same level as the married couples allowance. It is given in the year of her husband's death in addition to the full married couple's allowance. Widows bereavement allowance is also available in the following year. For 1998/99 the widows bereavement allowance is £1,900. This allowance is also restricted to 15%.

Blind Persons Relief – this applies to registered blind persons only. The allowance for 1998/99 is £1,330. This relief is given in addition to any other relief the person may be entitled to.

Pension Contributions

Pension contributions to approved schemes have special treatment. Although not a business expense, they are allowed as a deduction against taxable profits. There are, however, limits on the level of contribution permitted in any one year. We will concentrate on the rules applying to approved schemes that came into existence after 1 July 1988. These are known as personal pension plans. Schemes existing prior to this date are generally known as 'retirement annuities' and have different rules applying. You should take advice if you have any 'retirement annuity' schemes. Some people have both types of scheme. The rules governing their interaction for tax relief are very complex and, again, advice should be taken.

We will concentrate on personal pension plans. The level of contribution for tax relief purposes is dependent on two factors:

- your age at the beginning of each tax year (ie age on 6 April) *and*
- what are termed 'net relevant earnings' which we will discuss later.

The following table shows how much you can contribute for each age bracket.

Age on 6 April	Max % of Net Relevant Earnings
35 or less	17½
36–45	20
46–50	25
51–55	30
56–60	35
61–74	40

'Net relevant earnings' consists of the adjusted profit of the business (see example below) less any capital allowances or losses. There is, however, a ceiling to the amount of net relevant earnings that may qualify for relief in any one year. This is called the 'capping limit'. For 1998/99 this limit is set at £87,600 of net relevant earnings.

Example 1

Pat aged 47 made a profit for 1998/99 of £58,000. She had capital allowances of £12,000. What is the maximum pension contribution allowable?

	£
Profit	58000
Less Capital allowances	(12000)
Net relevant earnings	46000
Maximum pension contribution	£46,000 x 25% = £11,500

It is possible to elect, before the end of a tax year, to have a pension contribution paid in that year carried back to the previous year. It would then be treated as if it had been paid in that year. As a concession from the Inland Revenue, this time limit can be extended to 5 July following the end of the tax year .

Where there is an excess of relief available in any tax year (eg pension contributions paid are less than the possible contribution) then that excess can be carried forward for up to six tax years. The difference between the actual contributions paid and the maximum possible contributions is called 'unused relief'. Consider the following example.

Example 2

John born 1/1/42 had profits of £49,000 for 1998/99. He had capital allowances of £5,000. For the previous six years, John had the following profits and capital allowances. He paid the contributions shown into his pension scheme.

Year	Age at 6 April	Profit £	Capital Allowances £	Contribution Paid £
1992/93	50	19000	8000	2000
1993/94	51	20000	9000	3050
1994/95	52	28000	7000	6000
1995/96	53	30000	6000	4000
1996/97	54	32000	5000	5000
1997/98	55	42000	4000	9000

Let us work out the 'unused relief' available to carry forward to 1998/99.

Year	Net Relevant Earnings £	% Limit	Max Cont	Paid £	Unused Relief £
1992/93	11000	25	2750	(2000)	750
1993/94	11000	30	3300	(3050)	250
1994/95	21000	30	6300	(6000)	300
1995/96	24000	30	7200	(4000)	3200
1996/97	27000	30	8100	(5000)	3100
1997/98	38000	30	11400	(9000)	2400
			Total Unused Relief		10000

If John paid a premium of £20,400 in 1998/99, the position would be:

Year	Net Relevant Earnings £	% Limit	Max Cont	Paid	Unused Relief Utilised
1998/99	44000	35	15400	(20400)	5000

The maximum pension contribution that John can pay for 1998/99 is £15,400. Any contribution over and above this limit must be set against unused relief. John has £10,000 worth of unused relief available. Because of the six year carry forward rule, it makes sense to use relief from earlier years first. In this instance, John is utilising £5,000 of unused relief allocated as follows.

	£
1992/93	750
1993/94	250
1994/95	300
1995/96	3200
1996/97	500

Only £500 of the relief available for the 1996/97 tax year has been used. This leaves £2,600 which can be carried forward for up to six years. The unused relief of £2,400 for the 1997/98 year is also available to carry forward for up to six years.

Income Tax Rates

The rates shown below apply to taxable income, *ie income over and above your personal allowances*. Rates for 1998/99 are:

First £4,300 of taxable income	taxed at 20%
Income between £4,301 and £27,100	taxed at 23%
Income over £27,100	taxed at 40%

Example 3

For this tax calculation example, use the following information:

(i)   assessable profit figure from page 11 of £59,250
(ii)   pension contributions of £2,000
(iii) married couples allowance is due.

	Income £	Tax £
Assessable profit	59250	
Less personal allowance	(4195)	
Less pension contributions	(2000)	
	53055	
First £4,300 taxed @ 20%	4300	860.00
	48755	
Next £22,800 @ 23%	22800	5244.00
Remainder taxed @ 40%	25955	10382.00
Total tax payable		16486.00
Less tax credit for married couples allowance* £1,900 @ 15%		(285.00)
		16201.00

Notes:

* We mentioned on page 12 that the married couples allowance can only be relieved at 15%. The Inland Revenue will turn the married couples allowance into a 'tax credit' to be deducted from the total tax bill. In the example above, we can see that we have deducted £285 from the total tax bill, ie:

    the married couples allowance of £1,900 @ 15% = £285

Exercise 2

How much tax would a single woman with a child pay if she had taxable profits of £26,000 in 1998/99?

Check your answer with page 158.

How are Profits Assessed?

Before we can understand how profits are assessed for tax, we need to understand a couple of basic terms:

The business's accounting year

This is the 12 month period for which accounts are prepared. You can choose any year end which appeals to you. For example, you may wish to choose 31 December to coincide with the calendar year. Alternatively, you may choose a quiet trading period so that you have plenty of time to prepare the records for the accounts. If you have a business which has a high level of stock, you may wish to pick a quiet trading period when stock levels are relatively low in order to make the annual stock-take easier. Your first 12 month's trading is unlikely to terminate on your chosen accounting date by chance. However, your first accounting year can be longer or shorter than 12 months if you require. This will bring you up to the accounting year end date which you have chosen.

The fiscal or tax year

For purely historical reasons, the Inland Revenue has its own 'accounting year'. This commences on 6 April of each year and finishes on 5 April of the following year. This is why tax years are always labelled with two years, eg 1998/99. This means that the tax year commencing on 6 April 1998 will finish on 5 April 1999. The fiscal or tax year is also referred to as 'the year of assessment'.

The Taxation System

A new method for taxing profit was introduced for businesses that commenced after 5 April 1994. We will call this the 'new system'. For businesses that commenced on or before 5 April 1994, a different system of calculating profit was used and special transitional rules were introduced to switch them to the new system. We will call this the 'old system' and details of this, along with the transitional rules, can be found in Appendix 5 on page 179.

The New System

Under the new system, business profits are taxed in the same tax year as the accounting year end. The following diagram shows a business with an accounting year end date of 30 April 1998. The date ends in the 1998/99 tax year (which runs from 6 April 1998 to 5 April 1999) and any profits will become taxable in this tax year. This system is called the 'current year basis'.

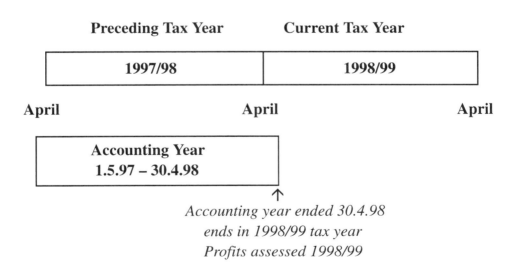

Opening Years (under the new rules)

There are rules concerning the first two years of trading. This is because the first year's accounts may span two tax years.

- The first tax assessment is based on the profits from the time the business commenced to the following 5 April.

- The second tax assessment is based on the profit of the first 12 months trading.

- The third and subsequent assessments are based on the profit of the accounts year which ends in the same tax year (as shown in the diagram on page 19).

Let's look at an example of a business which commences on 1 January 1997 and prepares its annual accounts to 31 December in each year. The profits for the two years ended 31 December 1997 and 31 December 1998 are as follows.

Example 4

| Year ended 31 December 1997 | Taxable Profits | £12,000 |
| Year ended 31 December 1998 | Taxable Profits | £15,000 |

The taxable profits would be divided for tax purposes as follows:

Tax Year	Accounting Period	Profit Assessed	
1996/97	1.1.97 to 5.4.97	£3,000	(ie 3/12 x £12000)
1997/98	1.1.97 to 31.12.97	£12,000	(ie first 12 month profits)
1998/99	1.1.98 to 31.12.98	£15,000	(ie year ended 31.12.98 ends in 1998/99 tax year)

Have a go at the following exercise yourself.

Exercise 3

John starts in business on 1 June 1996 and prepares his annual accounts to 31 May each year. His assessable profits for the year ended 31 May 1997 were £24,000 and for the year ended 31 May 1998 £26,000. Work out the assessable profit for tax years 1996/97, 1997/98 and 1998/99. Use whole months, ie ignore the five days to 5 April.

Tax Year	Accounting Period	Profit Assessed
1996/97		
1997/98		
1998/99		

Check your answer with page 158.

A detailed diagram showing the rules for the opening years for businesses commencing after 5 April 1994 (which is when the current year basis of taxation was introduced) is shown on page 22.

As you can choose your own accounting date, your first year's accounts may be longer or shorter than a twelve month period. There are special rules covering the assessment of profit in the early years of trading in these circumstances. These rules are explained in Appendix 4 on page 175.

OPENING YEARS

(Businesses commencing after 5 April 1995)

Business starts 1 May 1995
Accounting made up to 30 April annually

April 5	April 5	April 5	April 5
TAX YEAR 95/96	TAX YEAR 96/97	TAX YEAR 97/98	TAX YEAR 98/99
April 5	April 5	April 5	April 5

1st Trading Year
Apportioned

1 Jan 96 → 1 Jul 96

1st Trading Year

1 Jan 97 → 1 Jul 97

2nd Trading Year

31 Jan 98 → 31 Jul 98

3rd Trading Year

31 Jan 99 → 31 Jul 99

(Balancing payment 1997/98 due 31.1.99)
(Balancing payment 1998/99 due 31.1.2000)

Tax payment dates shown →

Period 1.5.95 to 5.4.96
Assessable Year 1995/96

Period 1.5.95 to 30.4.96
Assessable Year 1996/97

Period 1.5.96 to 30.4.97
Assessable Year 1997/98

Period 1.5.97 to 30.4.98
Assessable Year 1998/99

As we can see from the two examples above, the first year's business profits have been used to form the basis of two years' tax assessments. In John's case (Exercise 3 – page 21), the profits from 1 June 1996 to 31 May 1997 have been used to compute the taxable profit for both 1996/97 and 1997/98. These profits have, therefore, been counted twice. This doubly assessed period of profit has been called the 'period of overlap' by the Inland Revenue. The Inland Revenue recognises that it is unfair to tax businesses on the same profit twice and, therefore, tax relief will be given for the doubly assessed or 'overlap profits'. This relief is available on the earlier of:

– a change in the business accounting date that results in an accounting period of more than 12 months, *or*

– at the cessation of the trade.

In this book, we will not examine the change of accounting date as this can be a complicated procedure which should only be undertaken on the advice of an accountant. However, if overlap profits are used on cessation of trade, the amount of doubly assessed profit may have been eroded by inflation and, therefore, may be worth far less than when originally doubly taxed. Unless provisions are announced for increasing overlap profits to account for inflation, it may be worth using them as soon as possible by changing the accounting date. Take advice! Here's a tax tip – if you want to avoid the 'period of overlap', set your first accounting date to end on the following 5 April.

Self Assessment

Self assessment was introduced from the 1996/97 tax year. Under self assessment, the Inland Revenue set a 'filing date' by which Returns must be submitted. The 'filing date' is 31 January in the tax year after the tax year to which the Return applies. For example, the 1997/98 Tax Return covering income between 6 April 1997 to 5 April 1998 will need to be filed with the Inland Revenue by 31 January 1999. It will include profits of the accounting year ended during the 1997/98 tax year together with any other income, eg investment income earned between 6 April 1997 and 5 April 1998.

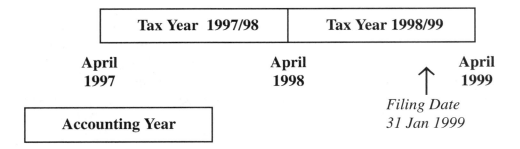

However, if the Return is issued after October 1998, it will be due within three months of the date of issue. If you trade as a partnership, you will have to include, within the Return, your personal share of the partnership profit.

Each Return to the Inland Revenue must include a 'self assessment' of any Income Tax and Capital Gains Tax due using the figures entered on the Return. This means that you will be required to work out your own taxation liability based upon the information you have stated in your own Tax Return.

However, for those who do not wish to work out their own tax bill, there will be the option of sending the completed Tax Return back to the Inland Revenue before 30 September following the end of the tax year. The Inland Revenue will then work out the tax due and raise the relevant assessment themselves.

Obviously, not everybody is a tax expert and, to make provision for this, the Inland Revenue have announced a facility under which the Inspector can amend the self-assessment to correct any obvious errors or mistakes within the Return. These will be known as 'repairs' to the Tax Return. Such repairs must take place within nine months of the date when the Return is delivered to the Inland Revenue. Alternatively, if you spot a mistake yourself after you have submitted the Return, you will also have the right to make an amendment to the Return provided you do this within 12 months of the date of submission to the Inland Revenue. You cannot do this if the Inspector has given you notice that your Tax Return is under enquiry. An Inspector has the right to enquire into any Tax Return providing notice is given within one year of the filing date of that Return.

Calculation of Tax Payments

Tax is paid on profit according to the tax year in which the accounting year ends. For example, if our accounting year were to end on 28 February 2000, we would pay tax based on the tax year commencing 6 April 1999 and finishing on 5 April 2000 (tax year 1999/2000). Tax on this year would be paid on 31 January 2000 and 31 July 2000 (with a balancing payment on 31 January 2001). Have a careful look at the diagram below. See if you can think of any problems that this method of tax collection could bring.

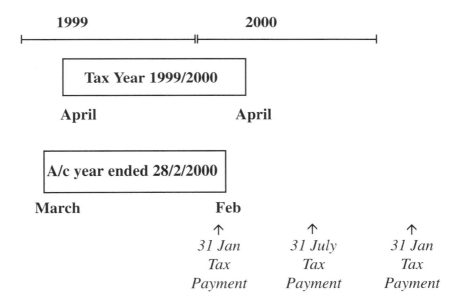

That's right! The first tax payment for the accounting year ended 28/2/2000 is payable on 31/1/2000. This means you are paying tax on profits of the year before you have finished trading for the year! How can you pay tax on a profit which you haven't yet calculated?

Well, the answer is simple – in effect, your January and July 2000 tax payments are only down payments against your total for the year ended 28/2/2000. Your final balancing payment takes place on 31 Jan 2001; this allows plenty of time for production of the accounts and final calculation of the actual tax owed to the Inland Revenue.

How does the Revenue work out the value of your down payments? Well, the rule is very simple indeed. Your two downpayments are set at half the level of tax that you paid in the previous tax year. Still confused? Here is an example showing how the system works.

Example 6

Assume that:

- Total tax due for accounting year ended 28/2/99 (which is assessed in tax year 1998/99) is £10,000.

- Total tax due for accounting year ended 28/2/2000 (which is assessed in tax year 1999/2000) is £16,000.

How would you pay tax for the tax year 1999/2000?
Let's start with a diagram which might make matters clearer.

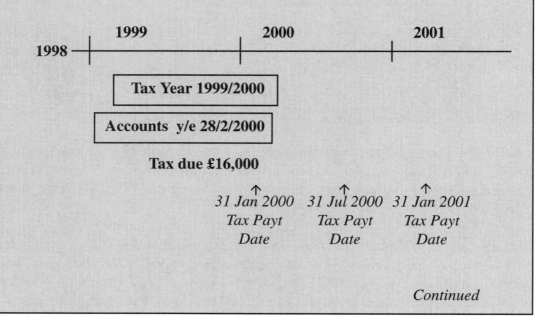

Continued

Example 6 (Contd)

Payments for the tax year 1999/2000 would comprise:

31/1/2000 'Downpayment' of half tax due for previous year (accounting
year 28/2/99 which falls in tax year 1998/99).
½ x £10,000 = £5,000

31/7/2000 'Downpayment' of half tax due for previous year (accounting
year 28/2/99 which falls in tax year 1998/99).
½ x £10,000 = £5,000

31/1/2001 Balance of tax due, viz:
Tax owed for tax year 1999/2000
£16,000 less 2 downpayments of £5,000 each
ie £16,000 - £10,000 = £6,000

Note: In addition to the balancing payment due on 31 January of £6,000,
you would also need to pay your first downpayment for the 2000/
2001 tax year. In this example, this would be half the 1999/2000
tax liability, ie £8,000.

Example 7

Calculate the amount of tax due for January for the 1999/2000 tax year given the following information.

1   Profit for the year ending 30 June 1999 is £50,000. This profit will be taxed in the tax year 1999/2000.

2   Total tax due for the 1998/99 tax year was £10,000 of which £6,000 has been paid leaving a balance of £4,000.

3   We don't know what 1999/2000 tax rates will be but, for simplicity, we will make the following assumptions.

-   Personal Allowance £5,000
-   Basic rate of tax 20% which applies on taxable incomes up to £25,000
-   Higher rate tax is 40%.

Payments Required Are:

By 31.1.2000
Balance of tax liability for 1998/99 (calculated as follows)

	£	£
Total liability	10000	
Less Payments on account made		
31 Jan 1999 & 31 Jul 1999	(6000)	
Balance now due	4000	4000
Plus Payment on account of income tax		
liability for 1999/2000 (calculated		
as half 1998/99 liability) £10,000 x 50% =		5000
Total due 31.1.2000		**9000**

Continued

Example 7 (Contd)

		£	£
By 31.7.2000			
2nd payment on account for 1999/2000			
(calculated as half 1998/99 liability)			
£10,000 x 50% =			**5000**

By 31.1.2001

			£	£
Balance of tax liability 1999/2000				
Profit	£50000			
Less Allowances	(£5000)			
Taxable profit	£45000			
Charge	£25000 @ 20% =	5000		
	£20000 @ 40% =	8000		
Total Tax due		**13000**		
Less Interim payments on account				
	31.1.2000	5000		
	31.7.2000	5000		
Balance due		**3000**	**3000**

		£
Plus 1st instalment 2000/2001, based on 50%		
of 1999/2000 tax liability £13,000 x 50% =		6500
Total Tax due		**9500**

The payment of tax must be made by the due date. The Inland Revenue propose to issue demand notes to remind people of the tax due. Non receipt of such a demand will not, however, be accepted as an excuse for not paying the required tax.

As the exercises show, the interim instalment will normally be based upon the previous year's income. Sometimes, profits will be on a declining trend. This means that tax payments based on last year's earnings may be too high. In this instance, the taxpayer can appeal to the Inland Revenue. The Inland Revenue will not have any power to challenge such a claim if it is reasonable at the time it is made. However, they will be able to impose a penalty for each instalment of up to 100% where it can be proven that people have deliberately reduced the interim payments to avoid paying tax by the due dates.

For the self-employed, this may produce a dilemma. The trader may know that the profits are dropping but cannot produce regular management accounts to prove it. Cash flow problems could arise by overpaying tax based on the previous year's tax liability. The alternative is to lodge an appeal to reduce the interim instalments. This risks a penalty for negligence if business fortunes improve prior to the accounting year end. This is where businesses producing regular management accounts score. They will be able to produce monthly management accounts which can be used to demonstrate to the Inland Revenue that the business is suffering declining profitability. Production of these accounts should constitute a strong defence against any subsequent Revenue claim for negligence should business profits show a strong upturn towards the end of the accounting year. Monthly management accounts are covered in the book called *Simple and Practical Accounting*.

Penalties

There are three main types of penalty under the new system. These penalties are:

- surcharges for late payment of tax
- penalties for delay in submission of Returns, and
- other penalties.

Surcharges

Surcharges will not normally apply to the interim instalments discussed above. However, if the total tax bill is not paid by 31 January following the year of assessment, then surcharges will definitely apply. These surcharges will be automatic unless a reasonable excuse for non payment is provided (which does not include the inability to pay). Provided tax is paid within 28 days of the due date, there will be no surcharge.

As the due date will be 31 January each year, payments made before 28 February will not attract a surcharge. However, they will incur an interest charge. If tax is paid between 28 days and six months after the due date, then an automatic penalty of 5% of the total tax due will be charged. If tax is paid more than six months after the due date, an automatic surcharge of 10% of the total tax will be charged. These surcharges will also attract interest if not paid.

Tax penalties

Delayed Returns

The penalty for late submission of Tax Returns will also be automatic unless a reasonable excuse can be shown. The Tax Return should be filed on 31 January following the tax year. If the Return is even one day late, a penalty of £100 will be charged. The Inland Revenue may also ask the General Commissioners for an additional penalty to be applied on a daily basis. If the Tax Return is more than six months late, the penalty will be £200. If the Tax Return is not submitted within 12 months after the original filing date, a tax related penalty of up to 100% of the tax can be sought by the Inland Revenue. For example, the 1998/99 Tax Return will be due to the Inland Revenue by 31 January 2000. If this is not submitted by 31 January 2001 then the Inland Revenue will have the power to charge an additional 100% of the total tax due.

Other Penalties

These mainly concern penalties for:

- failing to notify the Inland Revenue that a charge to tax has occurred, and
- failing to retain records to support the self assessment.

When income first arises, ie if you commence trading, you must notify the Inland Revenue by 6 October in the following tax year. Failure to notify the Revenue can result in a penalty of up to 100% of tax due.

When a self assessment is filed, ie on 31 January, records must be kept for one year regarding details recorded on the Return. However, in the case of a trade, or where letting income is involved, records must be kept for a period of five years following filing of the Return. The penalty for failing to retain records can be up to £3,000.

Interest

Interest will run on any tax which is not paid by the due date. Conversely, the Inland Revenue will pay interest on amounts of tax which are overpaid from the due date of payment to the date of repayment. Interest will also apply to the interim payments as well as the final payment and will run from the appropriate due date.

Losses

Hopefully, your business will not incur trading losses. If the business does, however, incur losses then the treatment of them for taxation purposes can be very complicated. Take expert advice if your business incurs a tax loss. However, here are a few guidelines.

In general, trading losses mean that:

- you don't pay tax on the trading year of the loss (since you don't have any profits to tax!)

- losses can be set against other income or capital gains of that year

- trading losses can be carried forward to be set against future profits, or

- trading losses can, in some circumstances, be carried back to profits of previous years.

Be aware that the rules are complicated. Either you need to do a great deal of work yourself in establishing what is allowed or, more practically, take professional advice.

Losses!

Opening and Closing Year Losses

There are special rules applying to losses made in the first four years of assessment for businesses. Losses in these years can be offset against income earned in the three previous tax years. This could be of particular significance to those who have paid Income Tax under Schedule E in the three years prior to starting their own business. *These people may be entitled to reclaim tax paid in their old job plus interest supplement!* This loss must be claimed however within two years of the loss being made. When a business ceases, if losses have been incurred in the last 12 months of the business then a special terminal loss relief is available. The relief is calculated by computing the loss during the final 12 months of the business – this loss is then available against trading profits during the tax year of cessation and of the three preceding tax years (giving relief against the later years in preference to the earlier years).

As stated previously, losses are a complicated area and this is definitely one where you need to take proper advice.

Schedule D Tax Planning

- **Don't let the tax 'tail' wag the business 'dog'**

  Remember, tax relief is normally worth 23% of any loss (40% at best). Never make a bad business decision to save 23% tax. You still bear the remaining 77% of the loss! Britain does not have high direct taxes.

- **Choice of Accounting Date**

  An accounting date early in the tax year, ie 30 April may be preferable. This gives you plenty of time to calculate your tax liabilities well before the payment dates. An accounting year end of 30 April is also good if your profits are rising as this will delay payment of tax on the higher profit for as long as possible.

  To avoid overlap profits, choose 5 April as your accounting date.

- **Opening Years**

  If you have business expenditure which can be incurred at any time, why not put it to best effect by using it in your opening year?

- **Opening Losses**

If you have paid a lot of Schedule E tax in previous employment and you have opening losses, check whether you can recover some Schedule E tax you have already paid.

- **Pension Contributions**

Don't get locked into fixed annual pension contributions (which you may not be able to afford every year). Make pension contributions flexible – if you have a good year, you may wish to invest a larger amount. This will:

  – increase your pension fund, and
  – reduce the tax on your profits.

- **Payment to Spouse**

Provided the work warrants it and your spouse has no other form of taxable income, pay your spouse for work performed in the business. This way, the marriage will attract an extra slice of personal allowance. The level of payment must be commensurate with the duties performed. Remember, if you are employing your spouse, you may have to register with the Inland Revenue for PAYE.

- **Spouse as Partner**

Provided you feel comfortable with the idea of your spouse as a business partner, you could attract an extra slice of tax relief by splitting the profits between you. This would be particularly worthwhile for very profitable businesses. Splitting the profit would minimise the effect of higher rates which would bear more heavily if only one person were to take all of the profit. However, your spouse's involvement in the partnership must be genuine and the allocation of profit should reflect the effort put in.

Exercise 4

Bill and Ben have operated a garage in partnership for some years. They have produced the following profit figure which they intend to submit to their local Tax Inspector. Do you have any advice to give them?

	£	£
Sales		260000
Cost of Sales		
Mechanics wages	80000	
Spare parts	40000	
Heat, light, power	6000	
		126000
Gross Profit		134000
Overheads		
Staff salaries	46000	
Owners drawings	22000	
Golf Club subscription	200	
Rent (garage)	1500	
Depreciation	2200	
Christmas gifts (Scotch)	160	
Staff party	380	
Staff pension fund	2400	
Partners pension fund	2200	
Wife's wages	1700	
Subsistence payments to staff	1650	
Redundancy payments	4600	
School fees	4000	
Theft by staff	1900	
		90890
Net Profit		43110

Continued

Exercise 4 (Contd)

Capital allowances of £1,900 are available. Partners' pension contributions are £1,100 each. Calculate their separate tax liabilities given that Bill takes 60% of the profit and Ben takes 40%? Both partners are married. All figures exclude VAT. Show your answers rounded to the nearest pound.

The pro forma below may help you with your calculations.

Bill and Ben (Answer Sheet)

	£	£
Net profit per accounts		
Add disallowed items:		
		———
Less:		
		———
Taxable Profit		
Profit Share	Bill (60%)	
	Ben (40%)	

Continued overleaf

Exercise 4 (Contd)

	Bill £	Tax £	Ben £	Tax £
Partner's share of profit				
Less				
Personal allowance				
Pension Contribution	_____		_____	
Tax @ 20%	_____		_____	
Tax @ 23%	_____		_____	
Tax @ 40%	_____		_____	
Total Tax	_____		_____	
Less Tax Credit for Marriage Allowance		(_____)		(_____)
Tax Payable		_____		_____

Check your answer with page 159.

Summary of Rates 1998/99

Personal Allowances

	£
Personal	4,195
Married Couple's	1,900 (Restricted to 15% relief)
Additional Relief for Children	1,900 (Restricted to 15% relief)
Widow's Bereavement	1,900 (Restricted to 15% relief)
Blind Person's	1,330
Age Allowance 65–74:	
– Personal	5,410
– Married Couple's	3,305 (Restricted to 15% relief)
Age Allowance 75 and over:	
– Personal	5,600
– Married Couple's	3,345 (Restricted to 15% relief)

Income Tax Rates

Taxable Income	Rate %
£1–£4,300	20
£4,301–£27,100	23
over £27,100	40

Introduction to VAT

Introduction

VAT stands for 'Value Added Tax'. It is an indirect system of taxation which enables the Government to tax consumer expenditure on a very wide scale.It covers most goods and services.

VAT replaced Purchase Tax when the United Kingdom joined the European Economic Community in April 1973. Its administration, collection and enforcement is the responsibility of HM Customs and Excise. Local VAT offices administer the scheme around the country. The Central Unit at Southend-on-Sea maintains a central record of registered persons, issues periodical VAT return forms and receives or makes tax payments.

What is VAT?

Although not an official definition, VAT could be described as:

'A tax on final consumer spending, collected in stages, when goods change hands or services are performed'.

Almost any business transaction can constitute a taxable supply for VAT purposes, eg:

- sale of goods
- performance of a service
- an exchange of goods or services, or
- a gift in kind

Wages paid to employees are not included.

Categories and Rates of Tax

There are three categories of VAT. These are exempt, zero rated and standard rate (fuel is an exception – VAT on domestic fuel currently stands at 5%).

Category	Examples	Rate
Exempt	Insurance Postal services Finance Education	No tax applies
Zero Rate	Food Children's clothes Books	Nil %
Standard Rate	Catering Adult clothing Footwear (In effect, any goods or services which are not in the previous categories)	17½%

The examples quoted above may appear to be definitive; in fact, there are exceptions for each example. It is important when supplying goods or services to make certain which category they are listed under. The General Guide to VAT (Notice No: 700) explains the scheme in considerable detail and should be referred to.

How VAT Works

VAT is collected at every stage in the distribution of goods and services by 'taxable persons'.

There are two aspects to VAT:

Input tax is the tax charged to you by your suppliers
Output tax is the tax charged by you to your customers.

Most traders will collect more tax from their customers than they pay to their suppliers. At the end of every quarter, they remit the surplus tax to HM Customs and Excise.

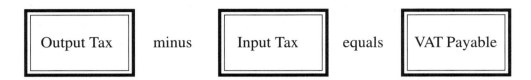

Occasionally, traders will pay out more VAT than they collect. In this case, they are entitled to a refund from HM Customs and Excise. Incidentally, traders who deal solely in zero rated goods will almost always get a refund! These people may find it worthwhile to opt for monthly VAT returns since they will get their money back quicker.

The diagram on page 45 shows how VAT is collected from a chain of four registered traders. Note that each trader is neither richer or poorer as a consequence of being VAT registered. Any surplus VAT collected by the trader is paid to HM Customs and Excise. Ultimately, the final (non registered) customer picks up the whole VAT bill.

VAT can be recovered on all items of business expense except for a special category called non-deductible inputs. This category includes motor cars purchased (other than for resale) and certain business and entertaining expenses. The cost to the business of non-deductible items is, therefore, the full cost price inclusive of Value Added Tax.

Obviously, accounting for input and output tax could be a real chore. Make sure that you have a sound book-keeping system which will do this efficiently. The *Book-keeping* workbook in the Simple and Practical series suggests various manual ways of keeping records. One of these methods will almost certainly suit you. Larger businesses may find the *Accounting with Computers* workbook more appropriate.

VAT Example

Trader	Costs		Sale Price excl VAT	VAT	Sale Price incl 17½% VAT	VAT Paid to HMC&E	
Supplier							
	Labour	£25				Output tax	£5.25
			£30	£5.25	£35.25	Input tax	Nil
	Profit	£5				VAT due	£5.25
Manufacturer							
	Material	£30				Output tax	£21.00
	Labour	£65	£120	£21.00	£141.00	Input tax	£5.25
	Profit	£25				VAT due	£15.75
Wholesaler							
	Material	£120				Output tax	£26.25
	Other	£10	£150	£26.25	£176.25	Input tax	£21.00
	Profit	£20				VAT due	£5.25
Retailer							
	Goods	£150				Output tax	£35.00
	Other	£30	£200	£35.00	£235.00	Input tax	£26.25
	Profit	£20				VAT due	£8.75
					Total Tax Paid by Customer	**£35.00**	

45

Who Has to Register?

A 'person' is required to register for VAT if:

- the value of their taxable supplies exceeds £50,000 in the last 12 months, or

- they *believe* that the value of their taxable supplies will exceed the annual limit in the next 30 days.

A 'person' is very widely defined; the definition includes self-employed individuals, partnerships, limited companies, clubs, associations or charities.

Registration covers **all** of the business activities of a person. A person is not allowed to fragment a large business so each activity falls below the current threshold. The threshold is normally changed annually in the budget. The limit was set at £50,000 from 17 March 1998.

You may register for VAT voluntarily even if your turnover is below £50,000. This will enable the business to recover VAT without waiting for the registration threshold to be reached.

Registration Procedure

- Persons who are required to register for VAT must apply on Form VAT 1 (or its Welsh equivalent). The completed form should be sent to the local VAT office.

- Where a partnership is concerned, Form VAT 2 must also be completed and forwarded with Form VAT 1.

- On receipt, the local VAT office will issue a 'Preliminary Advice of Registration' which will show a VAT registration number and effective date of registration.

- A person who fails to register for VAT is liable to a maximum penalty of 15% of the tax for which they are liable *or* to a penalty of £50, whichever is the greater. This penalty may, however, be mitigated depending on the reason for late registration.

The Tax Point

The 'tax point' is a very important date for VAT purposes as this determines the date upon which the supply of goods or services falls. This, in turn, determines the VAT quarter in which the trader has to account for the transactions. Tax points can be divided into two categories, the first being *basic* tax points and the second *actual* tax points.

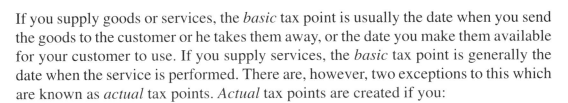

If you supply goods or services, the *basic* tax point is usually the date when you send the goods to the customer or he takes them away, or the date you make them available for your customer to use. If you supply services, the *basic* tax point is generally the date when the service is performed. There are, however, two exceptions to this which are known as *actual* tax points. *Actual* tax points are created if you:

- issue a tax invoice within 14 days after the basic tax point, the date you *issue* the tax invoice becomes the tax point, or

- if payments are made in advance of the date when the goods are removed or made available to the customer, then the *actual* tax point becomes the date of the invoice or payment.

It is, therefore, the tax point (not just the invoice date) which is used to decide in which quarter the VAT is to be accounted for.

The Tax Invoice

A tax invoice must be issued when VATable goods or services are supplied to another registered person. The following information is required by law on a tax invoice exceeding £100. Less detail is needed on invoices for supplies of less than £100 including VAT.

- an identifying number
- your name, address and VAT registration number
- the time of supply
- your customer's name (or trading name) and address
- the type of supply, eg sale, hire purchase, hire, sale on commission etc
- a description which identifies the goods or services supplied
- the total charge made, excluding VAT
- the rate of cash discount offered
- the total VAT payable.

For further details see Section VI of the *VAT Guide Notice 700* and also leaflet 700/21 *Keeping Records and Accounts*. It is essential for customers to retain all tax invoices in order to recover the VAT charged to them.

The Annual Accounting Scheme

Normally, a trader will complete the VAT Return based on the previous quarter's trading. Small firms, however, can elect to 'settle' their VAT account annually. There are two provisos:

- they must have been registered for 12 months and,
- they must have a taxable turnover below £300,000.

The trader is required to make nine equal 'standing orders' which are designed to clear the estimated liability. A final adjustment is made at the end of the year.

The Cash Accounting Scheme

This scheme allows registered businesses with an annual turnover below £350,000 to account for VAT on the basis of *payments* received and made, instead of *tax invoices* issued and received. Firms using the cash accounting scheme could show significant cash flow benefits as well as simplified paperwork.

Cash Accounting?

For one year only you can exceed the £350,000 limit. Providing that the turnover in that year does not exceed £473,500 and your turnover drops back to £350,000 in the following year you can continue on cash accounting throughout.

VAT Fraction

Some invoices and receipts do not show the amount of VAT separately. This is particularly true in the case of small purchases from retail outlets.

The formula for calculating the amount of VAT included in the total purchase price is:

$$\frac{\text{Rate of VAT}}{100 + \text{Rate of VAT}} = \text{Amount of VAT}$$

Assuming a standard rate of 17½%, the VAT fraction would be calculated as follows:

$$\frac{17.5}{100 + 17.5} = \frac{17.5}{117.5} = \frac{7}{47} \quad \text{of total invoice value}$$

The following example shows how to use the VAT fraction to calculate the amount of VAT contained in a VAT inclusive purchase of £117.50, assuming a VAT rate of 17½%.

$$\frac{7}{47} \text{ x £117.50} = \frac{822.50}{47} = \text{£17.50 VAT charged}$$

If the VAT had been shown separately, the invoice would have read:

Sale of goods	£100.00
VAT at 17½% of 100	17.50
Total invoice value	£117.50

Exercise 5

Assuming a VAT rate of 17½%, calculate how much VAT is included in the following VAT inclusive purchases. Check your answer with page 160.

(i) £176.25
(ii) £1186.75
(iii) £100

Completing the VAT Quarterly Return (Form VAT 100)

VAT Form 100 is issued by the Central Unit at Southend. Registered persons must complete the form and return it to Southend within one month of the end of the VAT quarter to which it refers, together with any payment due.

Failure to make a return, failing to pay tax or making false statements are all offences which may lead to punitive action by HM Customs and Excise.

Unless you are on the Cash Accounting scheme, base your VAT Return on the tax point *not* on the date that you actually receive or pay money. This means that you will normally pay tax on all invoices, receipts, bills, etc which bear a date falling within the VAT quarter, irrespective of whether the bills have been paid or not.

The main items of information required to complete the form are:

- output tax charged to customers
- input tax charged by suppliers
- value of sales exclusive of VAT
- value of purchases exclusive of VAT
- sales and purchase information relating to the EEC.

Exercise 6

Paul Jenkins runs his own business and submits VAT Returns for quarters ending 31 March, 30 June, 30 September and 31 December. He is not on the cash accounting scheme. The following information relates to the quarter ended 31 December. *All transactions have been carefully checked to ensure that the tax points fall in the correct quarter.*

Sales Invoices

Inv No	Inv Date	Tax Point	Value excl VAT
			£
100	15/10/97	18/10/97	6000
101	4/11/97	8/11/97	5000
102	1/12/97	1/12/97	12000
103	31/12/97	8/1/98	2500
			25500

Purchase and Expense Invoices

Inv No	Inv Date	Tax Point	Value excl VAT
			£
1	6/10/97	6/10/97	1300
2	2/11/97	5/11/97	1500
3	1/12/97	31/12/97	4000
4	11/1/98	24/12/97	6600
			13400

Calculate the VAT payable for the quarter ended 31 December 1997. Complete the VAT return shown on page 53 using the above information.

Check your answer with pages 161 and 162.

Value Added Tax Return

For the period

HM Customs
and Excise

For Official Use

Registration Number

Period

You could be liable to a financial penalty it your completed return and all the VAT payable are not received by the due date.

Due date:

For Official Use

Your VAT Office telephone number is

Before you fill in this form please read the notes on the back and the VAT leaflet *"Filling in your VAT return"*. Fill in all boxes clearly in ink, and write 'none' where necessary. Don't put a dash or leave any box blank. If there are no pence write **"00"** in the pence column. **Do not** enter more than one amount in any box.

For official use		£	p
VAT due in this period on **sales** and other outputs	1		
VAT due in this period on **acquisitions** from other **EC Member States**	2		
Total VAT due **(the sum of boxes 1 and 2)**	3		
VAT reclaimed in this period on **purchases** and other inputs (including acquisitions from the EC)	4		
Net VAT to be paid to Customs or reclaimed by you **(Difference between boxes 3 and 4)**	5		
Total value of **sales** and all other outputs excluding any VAT. **Include your box 8 figure**	6		00
Total value of **purchases** and all other inputs excluding any VAT. **Include your box 9 figure**	7		00
Total value of all **supplies** of goods and related services, excluding any VAT, to other **EC Member States**	8		00
Total value of all **acquisitions** of goods and related services, excluding any VAT, from other **EC Member States**	9		00

Retail schemes. If you have used any of the schemes in the period covered by this return, enter the relevant letter(s) in this box.

If you are enclosing a payment please tick this box.

DECLARATION: You, or someone on your behalf, must sign below.

I,..declare that the
(Full name of signatory in BLOCK LETTERS)

information given above is true and complete.

Signature..Date.............19......

A false declaration can result in prosecution.

L

VAT 100

53

Notes

These notes and the VAT leaflet *Filling in your VAT Return* will help you fill in this form. You may also need to refer to other VAT notices and leaflets.

If you need help or advice please contact your local VAT office.

If you are using the 'cash accounting scheme', the amounts of VAT due and deductible are for payments you actually receive and make, and not on invoices you receive and send out.

If you put **minus figures** in boxes 1 to 3 or are entering a sum **DUE** to Customs in box 4, please enclose the figure in brackets.

Amounts not declared correctly on previous returns

1. If any of your previous returns declared too much or too little VAT that has not yet been accounted for, you can correct the position using boxes 1 and 4 for net amounts of **£2000 or less.**

2. If the net amount is **over £2000**, tell your local VAT office immediately. Don't include the amount on this return.

If you do not follow these instructions you could be liable to a financial penalty.

How to pay your VAT

Cross all cheques and postal orders "AC Payee Only" make them payable to "H M Customs and Excise" and put a line through any spaces on the "pay" line.

In your own interest do not send notes, coins, or uncrossed postal orders by post.

If you wish to pay by 'credit transfer', ask your local VAT office. Pre-printed booklets of credit transfer slips will be sent to you.

Please write your VAT registration number on the back of all cheques and bank giro credit slips.

Where to send this return

You must make sure your completed form and any VAT payable are received by the 'due date' (shown over the page) by:
The Controller
VAT Central Unit
H M Customs and Excise
21 Victoria Avenue
Southend-on-Sea X
SS99 1AA.

Complaints

The Adjudicator reviews complaints not settled to your satisfaction by Customs. The recommendations of the Adjudicator are independent and the service is free. It covers complaints not general enquiries. [Telephone the Adjudicator on 0171 930 2292].

VAT 100

Box 1

Show the VAT due on all goods and services you supplied in this period.

Box 2

Show the VAT due (but not paid) on all goods and related services you acquired in this period from other EC Member States.

Box 3

Show the total amount of the VAT due ie the sum of boxes 1 and 2. This is your total **Output** tax.

Box 4

Show the amount of VAT deductible on any business purchases including acquisitions of goods and related services from other EC Member States. This is your **Input** tax.

Box 5

If this amount is under £1, you need not send any payment, nor will any repayment be made to you, but you must still fill in this form and send it to the VAT Central Unit.

Boxes 6 and 7

In box 6 show the value excluding VAT of your total outputs (supplies of goods and services). Include zero rated, exempt outputs and EC supplies from box 8.

In box 7 show the value excluding VAT of all your inputs (purchases of goods and services). Include zero rated, exempt inputs and EC acquisitions from box 9.

Boxes 8 and 9

EC TRADE ONLY
Use these boxes if you have supplied goods to or acquired goods from another EC Member State. Include related services such as transport costs where these form part of the invoice or contract price. The figures should exclude VAT.

The other EC Member States are: Belgium, Denmark, France, Germany, Greece, Netherlands, Ireland, Italy, Luxembourg, Portugal, Spain, Austria, Finland and Sweden.

You must tell your local VAT office about any changes in your business circumstances (including changes of address).

Bad Debts

From 1 April 1993, relief is available for bad debts six months after the time of supply. A VAT registered trader can claim a refund of output tax where:

- goods have been sold and VAT on the supply has been paid
- title to the goods has passed to the customer
- the receipt (or part of the receipt) for the supply has been written off in the accounts as a bad debt.

Scale Charges for Vehicles

In general, input tax on fuel purchased for business use is reclaimable. However, many vehicles used for business are also used privately. Obviously, you cannot reclaim the VAT on private use of business fuel. It is difficult to determine the level of private use unless a detailed mileage log is kept. To avoid keeping a mileage log, HM Customs and Excise have set an annual scale charge which can be used to account for VAT on private fuel.

The scale charges shown on the table below apply from 6 April 1998. They cover a three month period. The scale charge is added to the business output tax for every vehicle with private use. Note that the scale charge varies according to whether the vehicle uses petrol or diesel.

Cylinder capacity of vehicle	Scale charge diesel £	VAT due per car £	Scale charge petrol £	VAT due per car £
1400cc or less	196	29.19	212	31.57
More than 1400cc but not more than 2000cc	196	29.19	268	39.91
More than 2000cc	248	36.93	396	58.97

When completing your VAT Return, add the VAT due per car to the output tax figure. Also add the scale charge less the VAT due to Box 6 of the VAT Return – this records the total value of outputs, excluding VAT. For example, if you had a petrol car of 1400cc or less, the VAT output tax to be added would be £31.57. The amount to be recorded in Box 6 would be the total scale charge of £212 less the VAT charge of £31.57, resulting in a net of VAT figure of £180 (rounded) to be added to Box 6.

Although the scale charges shown in the table above apply from 6 April 1998, they relate to the *next* VAT accounting period beginning on or after 6 April 1998. The VAT scale charge, therefore, applies to the first clear quarter arising in the new tax year. There is no need to apportion scale charges between quarters.

Special Schemes for Retailers

There are nine special schemes for retailers which are designed to suit a variety of retail businesses. If your business is in the retail trade, check with your accountant or VAT office to see if any of these schemes suit your needs.

Trade with the EEC

From 1 January 1993, there was a change in the rules governing VAT accounting for businesses which export or import goods to or from another EC state. Advice should be taken if your business expects to export or import goods from these countries.

VAT Records

- A taxable person must keep a record of all transactions and related documents connected with their business operations.

- A taxable person must keep records and accounts up to date and is legally obliged to preserve them with all related documents for six years.

VAT Penalties

Penalties can be imposed for:

- late registration
- serious misdeclaration
- persistent misdeclaration
- tax evasion
- failure to keep or produce VAT records
- unauthorised issue of tax invoices
- breaches of most of the other requirements under VAT law.

HM Customs and Excise can also charge 'default interest' on underdeclarations and overclaims of VAT. Penalties can be severe.

Prompt and correctly completed returns and payments are the best way of avoiding trouble. In the event of problems, it may pay to enter into early discussions with your local VAT office.

Useful Information

All of the foregoing can be found in the following Notices:

The VAT General Guide	Notice No: 700
Should I be Registered for VAT?	Notice No: 700/1/92
The Ins and Outs of VAT	Notice No: 700/15/91
Filling in your VAT Return	Notice No: 700/12/93
Keeping Records and Accounts	Notice No: 700/21/91

A selection of useful VAT Notices is listed in Appendix 1 (page 141).

Requests for Notices and all queries regarding VAT should be made to your local VAT office. The address and telephone number is listed under 'Customs and Excise, Value Added Tax'.

VAT Rates Summary 1998/99

VAT rate	$17\frac{1}{2}\%$
VAT fraction	7/47
Registration threshold	£50,000
Deregistration threshold	£48,000
Cash accounting limit	£350,000
Annual accounting limit	£300,000

Chapter 4

Pay As You Earn (PAYE)

Introduction

Pay-as-you-earn (PAYE) was devised by government to make tax collection more efficient. PAYE enables the Inland Revenue to collect tax at regular intervals, usually weekly or monthly. It prevents tax payers facing heavy tax demands some time after the income has been received.

PAYE is a system of collecting tax from wages, salaries, commissions and bonuses etc. It applies to all employed persons. The rules for PAYE are contained within Schedule E.

Who Are My Employees?

Normally, it is obvious whether someone is an employee or not. However, be careful when dealing with people who claim to be self-employed but spend a great deal of time with you. The Revenue could decide to ignore their self-employed status and treat them as your employee. This is important because you become liable for their tax bills if they don't pay up themselves. Inland Revenue booklet IR56 will help you to decide on a person's employment status.

Employed or self-employed?

People who are self-employed generally:

- decide their own hours of work
- decide where to work
- can either do the job themselves or send a substitute
- provide their own equipment
- have their own business organisation, however small.

People who are employed generally:

- have a contract of employment
- are entitled to holiday pay, overtime and sick pay
- work under closer supervision by the management.

What is Pay?

From a tax point of view, pay is more broadly defined than may, at first, appear. For example, 'pay' includes:

- salaries
- wages
- fees
- overtime
- bonus payments
- commission
- pensions received
- sick pay
- statutory sick pay
- Christmas boxes
- tool allowance (building trade)
- vouchers exchangeable for cash
- payments for travelling time
- certain cash payments for meals
- payments in lieu of benefits in kind

- round sum allowances
- honoraria (voluntary payments for services supplied)
- employees' tax payments paid by the employer
- travel payments for journeys from home to work and back
- lump sum payments on certain retirement or removal from office
- gratuities or 'service charges' paid by the employer
- maternity pay and other payments made under the Employment Protection Act.

Pay does **not** include:

- Reimbursement of expenses provided that the expenses were necessary for the business.

- Rent free accommodation provided because of the nature of the job. This extends to free board and lodgings made available by the employer (provided the employee cannot opt for a cash sum in place of free board and lodgings).

Ideal rent free accommodation!

- Lodgings or 'away from work allowances' provided that they are no more than reasonable payments for the extra living expenses incurred by employees employed temporarily away from home and their normal place of employment.

- Meal vouchers which comply with certain conditions.

- Payments in lieu of notice.

- Benefits under the Workmen's Compensation Acts.

- Relocation and removal expenses borne by the employer where the employee has to change residence on first taking up the employment. This also applies to a transfer to another post within the employer's organisation. These payments are tax free up to a limit of £8,000.

- Payments into approved pension schemes are not included in gross pay.

Employers' Responsibilities

Employers are required by law to deduct income tax (and national insurance) from their employees' wages. The tax deducted in one month must be paid over to the Inland Revenue by the 19th day of the following month. Failure to deduct tax from an employee could make the employer liable to pay the tax himself. In serious cases, there could be penalties also!

The employer must keep a record of all employees' earnings and deductions in a form acceptable to the Revenue. The Revenue provides tables and deductions working sheets free of charge, together with a range of explanatory booklets. Should you elect not to use the stationery provided, you must use an approved alternative.

At the end of every tax year, the employer must inform the Inland Revenue of the:

- earnings of all employees
- tax deducted from all employees
- the total tax deducted and due to the Revenue
- the total tax paid to date.

This is done using forms P14 and P35.

At the end of each tax year, the employer must also submit a form P11D showing the value of any expenses or benefits (in cash or in kind) paid to employees earning more than £8,500 including the value of any benefits. Examples of benefits include company car, free fuel, beneficial loans, home telephone payments etc. A form P9D must be submitted for all employees receiving expenses and benefits, who earn less than £8,500.

Failure to submit the above documents within strict time limits can lead to heavy penalties and interest charges. From 1995, these penalties are automatic! The main due dates and penalties are as follows:

Date	Comment	Penalty/Interest
19/4/98	Date by which all PAYE tax and National Insurance contributions for 1997/98 should be made.	Interest accrues on all tax and NI paid after 19/4/98 to date of payment.
19/5/98	End of year documents P14 and P35 etc to be submitted to the Inland Revenue (legal requirement).	An automatic penalty will be imposed where a 1997/98 return arrives later than 26/5/98. The penalty is £100 a month for every 50 employees (or under) for each month or part month the returns are late. If returns remain outstanding for more than one year, a penalty of 100% of the tax and NIC due on 19/5/98 can be levied. Any incorrect return can result in a penalty of 100% of the tax and NIC underpaid.
19/6/98	Class 1A NICs due for 1997/98 (see later chapter on national insurance).	Interest accrues from 19/6/98 if not paid.
6/7/98	Forms P11D and P9D for 1997/98 to be received by the Inland Revenue.	The late returns are subject to a penalty of £300 per form plus up to £60 per day per form if the delay continues. An incorrect return is subject to a maximum penalty of £3000 per form.
30/9/98	Self assessment returns to be submitted to the Inland Revenue where individuals require the Revenue to work out the tax liability.	No penalty/interest consequences (optional).
31/1/99	Self assessment returns due for 1997/98 to be received by Inland Revenue.	Late or incorrect returns can be subject to interest and penalties.

The Revenue/DSS may inspect an employer's records at any time. Records must be kept for a period of at least three years. Appendix 1 (pages 139 and 140) contain a list of common Inland Revenue and DSS forms.

How Does PAYE Work?

Income tax can be calculated by hand, or by computer using a special payroll programme. This chapter will show you how to do the calculation manually. To operate PAYE, you will need:

– One P11 per person (see illustration on pages 72 and 73).

– A copy of *The Employers Quick Guide to PAYE and NICs CWG1 (April 1998)*. This is a set of 22 well written instruction cards for PAYE and National Insurance.

– A set of *Taxable Pay Tables (Tables LR + B to D)*.

– A copy of the *Pay Adjustment Tables (Tables A)*.

– A copy of the *Employer's Further Guide to PAYE and NICs CWG2 (1998)*.

– A knowledge of the employee's tax code.

The employee's tax code is agreed between the employee and the Inland Revenue as a consequence of information supplied on the employee's annual tax return – Form 11. The Inland Revenue notifies the employer of the employee's tax code on form P6. An employee's tax code is the amount of wages he/she is allowed to earn free of all income tax with the final digit removed, eg:

Employee's tax free income   £4195
Employee's tax code   419

Tax codes arrive with a range of prefixes and suffixes as follows:

- a code of one or more numbers followed by the suffix H, L, V, P or T
- a code with a prefix D
- a code with a prefix K followed by one to four numbers
- code BR
- code NT
- emergency code.

For the moment, we will only consider the first type of code, ie those comprising a series of numbers followed by the letters H, L, V, P or T. These are the most common types. The suffix has a significance as follows:

H   –   higher allowance; this is the married person's allowance
L   –   lower allowance; this is the single person's allowance
P   –   age allowance for a single person
V   –   age allowance for a married couple
T   –   other allowance *or*
         employee requests confidentiality.

To make manual calculations easier, the Revenue provides two sets of tax tables. The first set is used to calculate the amount of tax free pay. These are called *Pay Adjustment Tables* or, more simply, Tables A. Examples of Tables A are shown on pages 144 and 145.

The other set is used to calculate the amount of tax due on the taxable portion remaining. These are called *Taxable Pay Tables LR and B to D*. Examples of *Table LR* (LR stands for lower rate) and B, C and D are shown on pages 146 to 151. We will now do an example showing how to use these tables.

Example 8   How to Calculate Income Tax Owed

See the Deductions Working Sheet P11 on pages 72 and 73. We have taken an imaginary employee called Bill Gates. Note the information to be completed at the top of the form and the dates in the centre columns.

Bill Gates started work on 6 April. He will be paid monthly, in arrears. We enter his details on the top of the form as shown. His tax code is 524H.

1   At the end of the first month, his pay is £1,100. This is entered in column 2 on the fourth line (opposite month 1).

2   Enter the total pay to date in column 3, ie £1,100. (This is the cumulative total pay for the tax year).

3   To calculate column 4a, look at the *Pay Adjustment Tables – Tables A* (see examples on pages 144 and 145) and find Month 1 Tables A – Pay Adjustment (which is near the end of the Inland Revenue's booklet). You will see that the tax codes on the left hand side of each column run from 0 to 500. Alongside each tax code is a 'Total pay adjustment to date' figure. For example, someone with a tax code of 100 would be allowed to earn £84.09 free of tax in the first month of the tax year.

Let's look up Bill Gates' tax code of 524. Notice that the code exceeds 500. You will see there is a box at the bottom of the page giving instructions for where the code exceeds 500.

Continued

Example 8 (Contd)

First subtract 500 from the tax code then look up the excess in the table. In our example, the code is 524. If we subtract 500, we are left with 24 which gives free pay of £20.75 in the table. We then add this to the total tax free pay on 500 to arrive at the total free pay in the month:

Tax Free Pay on 500	£416.67
Tax Free Pay on 24	20.75
Total Free Pay in Month 1	£437.42

Enter the figure of £437.42 in column 4a.

4   Deduct column 4a from column 3 and enter the total taxable pay to date in column 5, ie £1,100 – £437.42 = £662.58. Ignore column 4b totally for now.

5   We now need to calculate the tax due at the end of month 1. Because there are several rates of income tax, ie 20%, 23% and 40%, there are several tax tables. These are labelled *Taxable Pay Tables – Tables LR + B to D*. There are two tables at the front of the Taxable Pay Tables which tell us which table to use. One table is for weekly paid employees and the other is for monthly paid employees. The table for monthly paid employees is reproduced on page 146.

To calculate the tax due, take the total taxable pay of £662.58 shown in column 5 and check which table to use. Since Bill Gates is paid monthly, we need to look up the 'Pay at Monthly Rates' table (see page 146). Bill Gates' taxable pay in month 1 exceeds £359 (first column) but does not exceed £2,259 (centre column) which means we now need to turn to table B.

Continued overleaf

Example 8 (Contd)

6   Table B shows tax rates of 23% – see example on page 148. Note that there is no entry for £662.58. This means that we will have to break the amount into two elements of £600 and £62. These amounts yield tax payable as follows:

Tax on £600 =	£138.00
Tax on £62 =	£14.26
Total tax due =	£152.26

7   £152.26 represents the tax on £662, assuming that the *whole* of the tax was charged at 23%. However, remember that everyone is entitled to pay tax at 20% on the first £4,300 of taxable income. Clearly, the taxpayer has been overcharged and is entitled to some form of rebate. This rebate can be read off from Table B – Lower Rate Relief (see page 149). You will see that, for month 1, you need to *subtract* £10.76 from the value calculated so far. The tax due from Bill Gates will, therefore, amount to:

$$£152.26 - £10.76 = £141.50$$

Enter this amount in column 6. Since this is the first month of the tax year, you can enter the same amount in column 7. Ignore columns 6a and 6b for now.

This completes the first month's entries. Continue working out the deductions for the second month as follows.

Example 8 (Contd)

8 Enter the pay for the month, say £1,200, in column 2 for month 2.

9 Total pay to date in column 3 comprises this month's pay plus the previous month's pay, ie £1200 + £1100 = £2300.

10 Look up 'Table A – pay adjustment' for month 2, tax code 524 (see page 145). Enter the amount in column 4a, ie £874.84

11 Deduct column 4a from column 3 and enter the amount in column 5, ie £2300.00 – £874.84 = £1425.16. Check whether this amount falls within Table B (see page 146) – which it does.

12 Look up 'Taxable Pay Tables – Table B' and note the total tax due to date for taxable pay of £1,425.16. Enter this amount in column 6. The value is made up of the following amounts:

$$£322 + £5.75 - £21.51 = £306.24$$

Remember to deduct the lower rate relief!

13 To calculate the tax due this month, subtract last month's tax deduction, ie £141.50 from £306.24 and enter the difference in column 7, ie £164.74. This is the tax to be deducted from Bill Gates' May salary.

Deductions Working Sheet P11   Year to 5 April 19_____

Employer's name

Tax Office and reference

National Insurance contributions

For guidance on National Insurance and the completion of columns 1a to 1h see CWG1 'Employer's Quick Guide to Pay As You Earn and National Insurance Contributions' - card 9

For guidance on Statutory Sick Pay figures see leaflet CA30

For guidance on Statutory Maternity Pay figures see leaflet CA29

***or** contact the Employers Help Line - telephone number is in the CWG1*

At the top of each section in the NI Tables there is a letter, for example *A, B, C, D or E*. Copy that letter from the Table you use to the box bottom left overleaf - see ▼ overleaf. If the employee's circumstances change part way through a year the letter may change as well. Record all letters with separate totals for each table letter used. Remember to record under letter Y any Class 1a on the last line of the box at ▼.
See the CWG1 card 11 for further information and examples

Earnings recorded in column 1a should not exceed the Upper Earnings Limit

For employer's use	Earnings on which employee's contributions payable *Whole pounds only* 1a £	Total of employee's and employer's contributions payable 1b £	Employee's contribution payable 1c £	Earnings on which employee's contributions at contracted-out rate payable included in col. 1a *Whole pounds only* 1d £	Employee's contributions at contracted-out rate included in column 1c 1e £	Statutory Sick Pay in the week or month included in column 2 1f £	Statutory Maternity Pay in the week or month included in column 2 1g £	Statutory Maternity Pay recovered 1h £	Month no	Week no
										1
										2
										3
									1	4
										5
										6
										7
									2	8
										9
										10
										11
										12
									3	13
										14
										15
										16
									4	17
										18
										19
										20
									5	21
										22
										23
										24
										25
									6	26
										27
										28
										29
									7	30
	Total c/fwd	Total c/fwd	Total c/fwd	Total c/fwd	Total c/fwd	Total c/fwd	Total c/fwd	Total c/fwd		

P11(1997)

BMSD8/96

72

Employee's surname *in CAPITALS*	Gates	First two forenames	William John

National Insurance no.	Date of birth *in figures*	Works no. etc	Date of starting *in figures*
ZX 00 11 22 B	Day 17 / Month 03 / Year 44	None	Day / Month / Year

Tax code †	Amended code †		Date of leaving *in figures*
524H	Wk/Mth in which applied		Day / Month / Year

PAYE Income Tax

For guidance on completing this form see CWG1 'Employer's Quick Guide to Pay As You Earn and National Insurance Contributions'

- *Card 10 for general completion*
- *Card 12 specifically for K codes*
- *Cards 11 and 12 for examples using suffix and K codes*

Month no	Week no	Pay in the week or month including Statutory Sick Pay/Statutory Maternity Pay 2 £	Total pay to date 3 £	Total free pay to date (Table A) 4a £	K codes only — Total 'additional pay' to date (Table A) 4b £	Total taxable pay to date i.e. column 3 *minus* column 4a *or* column 3 *plus* column 4b 5 £	Total tax due to date as shown by Taxable Pay Tables 6 £	K codes only — Tax due at end of current period Mark refunds 'R' 6a £	K codes only — Regulatory limit i.e. 50% of column 2 entry 6b £	Tax deducted or refunded in the week or month Mark refunds 'R' 7 £	K codes only — Tax not deducted owing to the Regulatory limit 8 £	For employer's use
1	1											
	2											
	3											
	4	1100 00	1100 00	437 42		662.58	141 50			141 50		
2	5											
	6											
	7											
	8	1200 00	2300 00	874 84		1425 16	306 24			164 74		
3	9											
	10											
	11											
	12											
	13											
4	14											
	15											
	16											
	17											
5	18											
	19											
	20											
	21											
6	22											
	23											
	24											
	25											
	26											
7	27											
	28											
	29											
	30											

† If amended cross out previous code.

Ø If any week/month the amount in column 4a is more than the amount in column 3, leave column 5 blank.

Exercise 7

Calculate Bill Gates pay for June, July and August as follows:

Pay on	30 June	£1,400
	31 July	£1,250
	31 Aug	£1,500

Hint: In case you don't have access to a full set of pay adjustment tables, the following may be useful.

MONTH	TABLE A Code 524H Pay Adjustment
	£
1	437.42
2	874.84
3	1312.26
4	1749.68
5	2187.10

Tables LR and B to D are to be found between pages 146 and 151 of this workbook. Use these to work out the tax due.

Check your answer with page 163.

What About Leavers and Joiners?

In our example, Bill Gates was already on the payroll on the first day of the pay year. How do we handle people who arrive and depart part way through the year? Provided we know:

- how much a new joiner has earned so far this tax year
- how much tax he has had deducted so far this tax year
- his tax code

we have sufficient input to make next month's tax deduction.

This information is relayed from one employer to the next on a P45 form. For example, if Bill Gates were to leave on 8 June, we would complete his P45 as shown on page 76. We would send the top part (Part 1) to the tax office. We would give the other two parts (Parts 2 and 3) to Bill Gates to pass on to his next employer. The new employer would then be in a position to make income tax deductions as normal.

If an employee arrives without a P45 form, you should ask him to complete a P46 form. Guidance for this is given on cards 4 and 5 of the *Employers' Basic Guide to PAYE and NICs*.

Inland Revenue

Details of employee leaving work
Copy for Tax Office

P45
Part 1

	District number	Reference number
1 PAYE Reference	485	M492

2 Employee's National Insurance number

ZX OO 11 22 B

3 Surname (in capitals)

Gates   Mr *(Mr Mrs Miss Ms)*

First name(s) (in capitals)

William John

4 Leaving date (in figures)

Day	Month	Year
08	06	19 98

5 Tax Code at leaving date. *If Week 1 or Month 1 basis applies, write 'X'in the box marked Week 1 or Month 1*

Code: 524H   Week 1 or Month 1

6 Last entries on *Deductions Working Sheet* (P11) **Complete only if Tax Code is cumulative.** *Make no entry here if Week 1 or Month 1 basis applies. Go to item 7.*

	Week	Month.
Week or month number		2
Total pay to date	£ 2300	OO p
Total tax to date	£ 306	24 p

7 This employment pay and tax. ■*No entry needed if Tax code is cumulative and amounts are same as item 6 entry.*

Total pay in this employment £   p

Total tax in this employment £   p

8 Works number Payroll number

None

9 Department or branch if any

N/A

10 Employee's private address and Postcode

19 Acacia Avenue
Fareham
Hants Po16 4DQ

11 I certify that the details entered above in items 1 to 9 are correct

Employer's name, address and Postcode

Mainspring Ltd
14 Church Road
Fareham Hants Po20 2DH

Date

8 June 1998

To the employer

For Tax Office use

- Complete this form following the 'Employee leaving' instructions in the *Employer's Basic Guide to PAYE* (P8). Make sure the details are clear on all four parts of this form. Make sure your name and address is shown on Parts 1 and IA.

- Detach Part 1 and send it to your Tax Office.

- Hand Parts 1 A, 2 and 3 (unseparated) to your employee when he or she leaves.

- If the employee has died, write 'D' in this box and send all four parts of this form (unseparated) to your Tax Office immediately.

P45(1996)   CCO 2/95

K Codes

K codes came into effect from 6 April 1993. Following the increases in recent years in car scale charges, it is now common for individuals' taxable benefits to exceed their personal allowances. Under the old PAYE arrangements, this gave rise to an annual income tax underpayment which could not be collected until an assessment was issued some time after the end of the tax year. To avoid this problem, employees whose benefits exceed their personal allowances are given a 'K' code.

K codes work in a similar way to the normal suffix codes except that the code is *added* to pay instead of taken away. The K code consists of the prefix K followed by a number, eg K468. The number represents the amount of taxable pay that the employee has added to his/her Schedule E earnings. This allows the Inland Revenue to deduct the full amount of tax on benefits from salary throughout the year.

Under these arrangements, tax deductions may be excessive if pay fluctuates from one month to another. The amount of tax to be deducted, therefore, is subject to a restriction of 50% of gross pay. Employees subject to a K code had to budget for a drop in their take-home pay from April 1993.

K codes replace F codes which were previously given to pensioners whose state retirement pensions exceed their personal allowances.

K codes operate in a similar way to normal suffix codes. To illustrate the point, let us take another employee, called John Akers, who earns exactly the same salary as Bill Gates. He has a tax code of K426. His P11 is on pages 80 and 81 of this book.

1 Assume John Akers is paid £1,100 in month 1. Columns 2 and 3 are the same as before. Instead of deducting 'tax free' pay in column 4a, we now add 'additional pay' in column 4b. The amount of additional pay is found from the pay adjustment tables for month 1 as before (use K code 426).

2 The sum of the normal pay and the 'additional pay' is entered in column 5, ie £1,100 + £355.75 = £1,455.75.

3 Tax on £1,455.75 falls within Table B of the taxable pay tables. Tax due is calculated as:

Tax on £1400	£322.00
Tax on £55	12.65
	334.65
Less lower rate relief	10.76
Tax payable	£323.89

4 The maximum amount that may be deducted in any month is 50% of the pay of that month. This is a safeguard to prevent unusual circumstances taking all the employee's pay for that month! This is called the 'regulatory' limit, it is entered in column 6b. For John Akers, the regulatory limit is £550 for month 1.

5 John Aker's tax deduction is the lesser amount of columns 6a and 6b. In our example, this amounts to £323.89 which is the sum entered in column 7. We will deduct £323.89 from this month 1 pay to cover income tax.

6 Month 2 is calculated in a similar way to month 1. If John Akers is paid £1,200 in month 2, his cumulative pay will amount to £2,300 which is entered in column 3.

7   We can look up the additional pay for K426 in the pay adjustment tables for month 2, this amounts to £711.50.

8   We now *add* columns 3 and 4b to produce month 2 taxable income which is £3,011.50.

9   Tax on £3,011.50 for month 2 falls within Table B of the taxable pay tables. Tax for this month would amount to:

Tax on £3000	£690.00
Tax on £11	2.53
	692.53
Less lower rate relief	21.51
Tax for month 2	£671.02

10 Subtract the value in column 6 for month 2 from the value in column 6 for month 1 (£671.02 – £323.89) and put the result (£347.13) in column 6a.

11 The tax to be deducted from John Aker's salary is the lower of the regulatory limit (£600) and the value in column 6a (£347.13). We enter £347.13 in column 7.

Important Note: The 'additional pay' added to pay for PAYE purposes has no effect on either the employee's or the employer's liability for National Insurance contributions.

Deductions Working Sheet P11   Year to 5 April 19____

Employer's name
Tax Office and reference

National Insurance contributions

For guidance on National Insurance and the completion of columns 1a to 1h see
CWG1 'Employer's Quick Guide to Pay As You Earn and National Insurance
Contributions' - card 9
For guidance on Statutory Sick Pay figures see leaflet CA30
For guidance on Statutory Maternity Pay figures see leaflet CA29
***or** contact the Employers Help Line - telephone number is in the CWG1*

At the top of each section in the NI Tables there is a letter, for example *A, B, C, D*
or E. Copy that letter from the Table you use to the box bottom left overleaf - see ▼
overleaf. If the employee's circumstances change part way through a year the letter may
change as well. Record all letters with separate totals for each table letter used.
Remember to record under letter Y any Class 1a on the last line of the box at ▼.
    See the CWG1 card 11 for further information and examples

Earnings recorded in column 1a should not exceed the Upper Earnings Limit

For employer's use	Earnings on which employee's contributions payable *Whole pounds only* 1a £	Total of employee's and employer's contributions payable 1b £	Employee's contribution payable 1c £	Earnings on which employee's contributions at contracted-out rate payable included in col. 1a *Whole pounds only* 1d £	Employee's contributions at contracted-out rate included in column 1c 1e £	Statutory Sick Pay in the week or month included in column 2 1f £	Statutory Maternity Pay in the week or month included in column 2 1g £	Statutory Maternity Pay recovered 1h £	Month no	Week no
										1
										2
										3
										4
										5
										6
									2	7
										8
										9
										10
										11
										12
									3	13
										14
										15
										16
									4	17
										18
										19
										20
									5	21
										22
										23
										24
										25
									6	26
										27
										28
										29
									7	30
	Total c/fwd	Total c/fwd	Total c/fwd	Total c/fwd	Total c/fwd	Total c/fwd	Total c/fwd	Total c/fwd		

P11(1997)

BMSD8/96

Employee's surname *in CAPITALS*	Akers	First two forenames	John

National Insurance no.	Date of birth *in figures*			Works no. etc	Date of starting *in figures*		
PL 24 82 93 B	Day 19	Month 04	Year 40	None	Day	Month	Year

Tax code †	Amended code †				Date of leaving *in figures*		
K426	Wk/Mth in which applied				Day	Month	Year

PAYE Income Tax

For guidance on completing this form see CWG1 'Employer's Quick Guide to Pay As You Earn and National Insurance Contributions'
- Card 10 for general completion
- Card 12 specifically for K codes
- Cards 11 and 12 for examples using suffix and K codes

Month no	Week no	Pay in the week or month including Statutory Sick Pay/Statutory Maternity Pay 2 £	Total pay to date 3 £	Total free pay to date (Table A) 4a £	K codes only Total 'additional pay' to date (Table A) 4b £	Total taxable pay to date i.e. column 3 *minus* column 4a **or** column 3 *plus* column 4b 5 £	Total tax due to date as shown by Taxable Pay Tables 6 £	K codes only Tax due at end of current period Mark refunds 'R' 6a £	Regulatory limit i.e. 50% of column 2 entry 6b £	Tax deducted or refunded in the week or month. Mark refunds 'R' 7 £	K codes only Tax not deducted owing to the Regulatory limit 8 £	For employer's use
	1											
	2											
	3											
1	4	1100 00	1100 00		355 75	1455 75	323 89	323 89	550 00	323 89		
	5											
	6											
	7											
2	8	1200 00	2300 00		711 50	3011 50	671 02	347 13	600 00	347 13		
	9											
	10											
	11											
	12											
3	13											
	14											
	15											
	16											
4	17											
	18											
	19											
	20											
5	21											
	22											
	23											
	24											
	25											
6	26											
	27											
	28											
	29											
7	30											

† If amended cross out previous code.

Ø If any week/month the amount in column 4a is more than the amount in column 3, leave column 5 blank.

Exercise 8

Calculate John Akers pay for June, July and August as follows:

Pay on	30 June	£1,400
	31 July	£1,250
	31 Aug	£1,500

In case you don't have access to a full set of pay adjustment tables, you may find the following useful.

MONTH	TABLE A Code K426 Pay Adjustment
	£
1	355.75
2	711.50
3	1067.25
4	1423.00
5	1778.75

Tables LR and B to D are to be found between pages 146 and 151 of this workbook. Use these to work out the tax due.

Check your answer with page 164.

Other Codes

DO Codes

So far, we have used tax codes on a cumulative basis. Each wage payment has been added to previous payments and the tax calculated on the whole of the earnings year to date. 'DO' codes operate differently. Simply, take the earnings for the week or month and subtract tax at 40%. There are no allowances of any kind to take into consideration. This code generally means the employee has another source of income which uses up all their tax free allowances and their lower and basic rate bands for tax. Look at Table D on page 151. You will notice a series of columns labelled 'income' with a taxable amount alongside. To use the table, simply look up the gross wage and deduct the tax from the table.

Emergency Codes

This code can be used cumulatively or non-cumulatively. The emergency code is the single person's personal allowance. For 1998/99, this is £4,195. Emergency codes are used when a new employee does not give you a P45.

Code NT

Code NT is very simple. NT stands for 'no tax' which means that employees with this code have no income tax deducted from their wages at all.

Code BR

BR stands for basic rate. However much the individual earns, he will be taxed at the basic rate. At present, this rate is 23%. This means that you will use Table B (see page 148) whatever the earnings.

Statutory Maternity Pay

Qualifying Conditions:

To be entitled to statutory maternity pay:

- A woman must have been continuously employed by you for at least 26 weeks. This period must continue into the 15th week before the week the baby is due. The 15th week is known as the 'qualifying week'.

- To claim SMP, the average weekly earnings must exceed the lower limit for National Insurance Contributions (£64 per week 1998/99).

- The employee must still be pregnant 11 weeks before the baby is due, or have had the baby at that time.

- The employee must supply medical evidence of the date the baby is expected (Form MATB1 Maternity Certificate) from her doctor. This must be provided at least 21 days before maternity leave starts.

- The employee must have stopped working.

Rates of Maternity Pay

There are two weekly rates of SMP depending on length of employment. These are:

Higher rate: 90% of employee's average weekly earnings payable for first six weeks of SMP period. If, however, this is lower than the lower rate, the lower rate is paid.

Lower Rate: Set rate (£57.70 per week from 6 April 1998) which is reviewed each year and is payable for remaining weeks that SMP is due.

Payment of SMP

- SMP is payable for up to 18 weeks, even if the employee does not intend to return to work after the baby is born.

- The SMP period starts at any time from the start of the 11th week before the expected week in which the baby is due (the week of confinement). If the employee works up to the birth, SMP is due from the Sunday following the date of birth.

- SMP is subject to National Insurance Contributions and Income Tax in the same way as normal wages.

- All employers can recover 92% of gross SMP paid. Small employers who pay less than £20,000 Class 1 contributions in the previous tax year (excluding Class 1A contributions) can recover 100% of SMP paid. In addition to this, small employers can also claim compensation at 7% of the gross SMP to compensate for employer's National Insurance Contributions.

- The recovery of SMP is by deduction from monthly Income Tax and National Insurance contributions on all employees.

- The DSS produce guides and tables that will help you:

  - Understand the basic principles of SMP (see *Employer's Quick Guide CWG1 April 1998 card 17*).

  - Deal with special or unusual situations (see the April 1998 Supplement to the *Statutory Maternity Pay Manual For Employers CA29 from April 1997*).

  - Determine the qualifying week from which SMP is due, (see CA35/36 from April 1998).

Example 9

Jane, who is expecting a baby, has average weekly earnings of £145 per week. She has been employed continuously by Smith & Jones for five years.

Jane produces a certificate (MATB1) confirming the baby is expected on 17 October 1998.

We must establish:

  - the expected week of confinement (EWC)
  - the qualifying week (QW) for SMP purposes.

Refer to the table following, which is an extract from the DSS Tables CA36.

Continued

Column 1 Expected week of confinement (EWC)	Column 2 Qualifying week (QW) Commencing	Column 3 Latest start date for 26 weeks Sunday	Column 4 11th week before the EWC employment	Column 5 6th week before the EWC
04.10.98 to 10.10.98	21.06.98	03.01.98	19.07.98	23.08.98
11.10.98 to 17.10.98	28.06.98	10.01.98	26.07.98	30.08.98
18.10.98 to 24.10.98	05.07.98	17.01.98	02.08.98	06.09.98
25.10.98 to 31.10.98	12.07.98	24.01.98	09.08.98	13.09.98

We can see from the table, if the baby is due on 16 October 1998, the expected week of confinement starts on 11 October 1998 in Column 1. We can then read across to Column 2 which tells us that the qualifying week for SMP purposes commences on 28 June 1998.

Jane would therefore be entitled to SMP of:

Higher Rate: £145 x 90% = £130.50 pw for six weeks, and
Lower Rate: £57.70 pw for up to twelve weeks.

NB The table also has other important dates recorded as follows:

Column 3   Tells the employer the latest date by which employment must have commenced to enable SMP to be payable.

Column 4   Tells the employer the date on which the employee must still be pregnant for SMP to be due, *and*

Column 5   Tells the employer the last date for commencement of SMP payments if the employee has stopped work.

Statutory Sick Pay

Quick Guide

- Payable to all employees under age 65 who are sick for four or more days (including Saturdays, Sundays and Bank Holidays.

- Operated and paid by employer.

- The gross amount of SSP is subject to income tax under PAYE and national insurance contributions.

- SSP is payable for up to 28 weeks of sickness.

- A period of sickness is known as the 'period of incapacity for work' (PIW). If there is more than one PIW in a period of eight weeks or less, these are linked together for SSP purposes.

- The first three days of any PIW do not qualify for SSP purposes. These are known as waiting days.

- Qualifying days for SSP purposes are those days on which the employee is normally required to work, ie if the employee is required to work between Monday to Friday, there will be five qualifying days for SSP purposes.

- From 6 April 1995, employers may be able to recover a proportion of SSP paid under the percentage threshold scheme. The amount that can be reclaimed is any balance of SSP in excess of 13% of total employer's and employees' National Insurance payments during each month. For example, in June:

Total Class 1 NIC liability	£856.25
13% of £856.25 =	£111.31
Total SSP payments	£149.29
Amount recoverable	£37.98 (£149.29 - £111.31)

- SSP is recovered by reducing the NI contribution paid during the month on all employees. Where the SSP recoverable exceeds NI contributions due for a month any surplus is deducted as follows:

  – from PAYE tax payments made in the month
  – carried forward and deducted from the next payment period
  – reclaimed from the Collector of Taxes on application.

- The Statutory Sick Pay and Statutory Maternity Pay tables CA35/36 from April 1998 show the current rates of SSP in a ready-reckoner form. These tables also contain very useful 'linking' tables for PIWs.

- Refer to the employers SSP Manual CA30 from April 1997 (with April 1998 Supplement) before paying SSP. This will help:

  – you decide if SSP is payable
  – tell you how to compute average weekly earnings, *and*
  – tell you when to stop paying SSP to the employee.

- For employees with average weekly earnings of £64 or more, a single weekly rate of SSP is payable. For a PIW, the rate from 6 April 1998 is £57.70.

Let's look at an example. The tables for Statutory Sick Pay are reproduced on page 160.

Example 10

John has average weekly earnings of £235 and works for you from Monday to Friday. John is away sick from Sunday to the following Sunday. We will assume that there are no previous PIWs in the preceding eight weeks.

The first three qualifying days will be waiting days and Statutory Sick Pay will not be payable for these days. Therefore, Statutory Sick Pay will only be payable for Thursday and Friday, remembering that Statutory Sick Pay will not be payable for Saturday and Sunday as these are not qualifying days in John's case.

We would now refer to the table providing the daily rates of SSP payable (see page 156). We would then find the number of qualifying days in the week. John has five so we would find (5) in the 'number of qualifying days in a week' column. We have decided that Statutory Sick Pay is payable for two days so we would then move across to the column headed by (2). This gives us an amount of Statutory Sick Pay payable of £23.08. This would then be treated as earnings during the week and we would then calculate PAYE and National Insurance as per normal using the form P11.

Have a go at the following exercise yourself.

Exercise 9

Using the tables on Page 156, compute the Statutory Sick Pay payable for the following employees.

Assume that there are no linking PIWs in the previous eight weeks.

Employee	Average Weekly Earnings £	No of Qualifying Days in Week	Days Sick	SSP Payable in Week £
Jan	220	6	Sunday to Friday	
Joe	199	5	Sunday to Sunday	
Stuart	56	5	Tuesday to Friday	
Donna	136	4	Monday to Wednesday	

Check your answer with page 165.

Schedule E – Summary

☐ Make sure that you have all of the forms, literature and tables required. Appendix 1 (page 139) contains a list of common Inland Revenue forms.

☐ Learn your way around the *Employer's Quick Guide to PAYE and NICs*. This consists of a series of cards bearing the code CWG1 April 1998.

☐ If you still have problems, call your local Inland Revenue office and ask for 'PAYE' enquiries. In the author's experience, staff are very helpful indeed.

☐ If you are not working out the wages yourself, make an occasional check on the worksheets completed by your wages clerk. Occasionally, things can go off the rails with disastrous consequences.

☐ Ensure all payments and documents are submitted on time. This will avoid interest charges and penalties.

Chapter 5

National Insurance

Introduction

National Insurance is similar in nature to income tax. Like income tax, the more you earn the higher the rate of tax levied. Unlike income tax, there are no reliefs for personal circumstances (like marriage allowance). Tax is levied on the gross income *before* deduction of income tax.

National Insurance is divided into four classes. These are labelled Classes 1 – 4.

Class 1   is a tax levied on employed persons *and* their employers.

Class 1a   is a special contribution over and above Class 1 contributions which taxes private use of business cars.

Class 2   is a flat rate tax levied on the self employed. The self employed normally have to pay Class 4 contributions as well.

Class 3   is a voluntary tax which preserves state benefits for those who are not making contributions via their work.

Class 4   is a profits tax paid by the self employed. It is in addition to their Class 2 contributions.

These taxes are considered in more detail on the following pages.

Class 1 Contributions

Class 1 contributions are paid by employed persons *and* their employers. The only exceptions are employees on very low earnings. To avoid Class 1 contributions, the employee must earn less than the lower earnings limit which for 1998/99 is £64 per week.Below this figure, neither the employer nor the employee make Class 1 contributions.

Above the lower earnings limit, both parties are taxed according to the following table:

Class 1 – rates payable on all earnings 1998/99

Earnings per week	Contracted In		Contracted Out	
	Employer	Employee	Employer	Employee
£	%	%	%	%
64 – 109.99	3.0	*2/10	*3.0/0.0	*2/8.4
110 – 154.99	5.0	*2/10	*5.0/2.0	*2/8.4
155 – 209.99	7.0	*2/10	*7.0/4.0	*2/8.4
210 – 485	10.0	*2/10	*10.0/7.0	*2/8.4
over 485	10.0	£43.38	**10.0/7.0	£36.64

* on first £64
** on first £64 and on earnings in excess of £485
Employer's NIC of 10% payable on car benefits applicable to company cars and car fuel

Note that there are two rates depending on whether the employee is 'contracted in' or 'contracted out'. These are explained below.

Contracted In Contributions

No national insurance is paid provided the employee earns less than £64 per week. Once the £64 per week threshold has been reached, employees' and employers' contributions are payable on the *whole* of the earnings. For the employee, however, the rate applicable to the first £64 of earnings is only 2%. Earnings over £64 attract tax at the rate of 10% up to the upper earnings limit of £485. This means that no contracted in employee pays more than £43.38 per week, however much they earn. Note that there is no employer's ceiling. The employer has to pay Class 1 contributions on the whole of the earnings of the employee, no matter how high the salary.

Contracted Out Contributions

No national insurance is paid provided the employee earns less than £64 per week. However, once this threshold is reached, similar rules apply as for contracted in contributions. Note, however, that the rates are generally lower. This is because the employer (and possibly the employee) is also contributing to a private pension scheme. Again the employee pays only 2% of the first £64 of earnings. Earnings over £64 per week attract a slightly lower tax rate of 8.4%. The maximum that any contracted out employee can pay is £36.64 per week.

Note the different contribution rates for the employer's contributions. The employer pays a higher rate on the first £64 of contributions with a lower rate payable on any earnings above £64. There is no ceiling to the employer's contribution.

How to Calculate Class 1 National Insurance

Class 1 national insurance can be calculated by hand or by using a computerised payroll program. Calculation of the tax by hand is very straightforward. The government provides three types of National Insurance Tables. These are:

Table A (Standard rate)   is for 'normal' employees who make standard rate contributions.

Table B (Reduced rate)   is for married women and widows who hold a valid reduced rate certificate.

Table C (Pensioners)   is for employees over retirement age (65 for men and 60 for women). Note that the entire contribution is met by the employer; there are no employees' contributions in Class C.

Each table is available in two versions, one for weekly paid employees and one for monthly paid employees. Appendix 2 (pages 152 to 155) shows various examples. Take the following steps to calculate NI by hand.

- Prepare a P11 for your employee (including name, national insurance number, date of birth etc).

- Decide which table to use, ie Tables A, B or C – weekly or monthly version.

- Look up the employee's gross weekly or monthly pay in the table. If the exact amount is not in the table, take the next lowest figure.

- Turn to the example of Bill Gates' P11 on pages 72 and 73. Note that the left hand side is labelled 'National Insurance Contributions'. Note also the headings on the columns. Enter the gross wage in column 1a, the total of the employee's and employer's contribution in column 1b and the employee's contribution in column 1c.

Note: Company directors' national insurance contributions are worked out using a different method. If you have company directors, check the *National Insurance for Company Directors Manual, CA44(NI35) from April 1995.*

- Fourteen days after the end of each income tax month, you must pay the Inland Revenue all national insurance taken from employees during that month. Include all income tax deductions in the same payment. The Revenue provides special 'paying in' booklets which include details of how to make the payments.

- If your average monthly payments to the Inland Revenue are less than £600, you can elect to make the payments quarterly.

- At the end of each tax year, you need to send the Inspector of Taxes an end of year summary form (P14) for each employee and a P35.

Exercise 10

Calculate Bill Gates' Class 1 national insurance contributions between 6 April and 5 September. Remember his earnings were:

	£
April	1,100
May	1,200
June	1,400
July	1,250
Aug	1,500

Enter your answer on Bill's P11 (which is on page 72). Ignore Class 1A contributions. Use the tables on pages 152 and 153.

Check your answer with page 166.

If you have problems with calculating Class 1 contributions, check the introductory pages of the National Insurance tables (which are very helpful). For more detailed information, check the Employer's Manual (leaflet NI 269) and the 'Quick Guide' (NI 268). If you still have difficulty, you can call the advice line on 0345 143 143.

Class 1A Contributions

Employers are required to pay Class 1A contributions on the private use of business cars. This tax applies where an employee:

- earns more than £8,500 *and*
- has the use of a company car *and*
- has private use of that vehicle.

Calculations are based on:

- Car benefit (as assessed under the rules introduced on 6 April 1994)
- Fuel scale charges.

Car Benefit

The car benefit is 35% of the *original* list price of the car plus any additional accessories. The original list price applies irrespective of whether the car was bought with a discount. It even applies if the car was bought second hand. Any contributions towards the cost of the car by the employee may be deducted (up to a maximum of £5,000). The maximum list price is £80,000. There are discounts from this figure where:

- The employee drives more than 2,500 business miles per year. The benefit is reduced by one third.

- The employee drives more than 18,000 business miles per year. The benefit is then reduced by two thirds.

There is a *further* reduction of one third if the car is over four years old at the end of the tax year.

Let us consider an example.

Example 11

John's company car had an original list price of £10,000 and had additional accessories of £2,000 fitted. John completes 20,000 business miles a year and the car will be over four years old by 5 April 1999. The benefit would be calculated as follows:

List price of car	£10000		
Accessories	2000		
Total cost	£12000		
Car benefit is £12000 x 35%		=	4200
Less Discount for high mileage 2/3		=	(2800)
			1400
Less Discount for age 1/3		=	(467)
Total benefit			933

Fuel Benefit

The fuel benefit scale charges must be added to the car benefit when working out Class 1A contributions. This applies where an employee is provided with fuel for private use. For 1998/99 the annual fuel benefit scale charges are as follows:

PETROL		DIESEL	
Engine Size	**Scale Charge**	**Engine Size**	**Scale Charge**
	£		£
0 – 1400cc	1010	0 – 2000cc	1280
1401 – 2000cc	1280		
2001cc +	1890	2001cc +	1890

Class 1A contributions for the tax year 1998/99 are payable on 19 July 1999. Remember to apply the Class 1A national insurance rate for the year of *use* not the year of *payment*.

A car benefit?

Let us work out the Class 1A contributions payable on John's car for 1998/99 assuming:

- John is provided with fuel for private use
- the car is a petrol vehicle
- the car has a 1600cc engine.

Car benefit as previously calculated	933
Add fuel benefit	1280
Total benefits	2213

Class 1A contribution = £2213 x 10% = £221.30

Class 1A contributions do not relate to trucks, vans or lorries but they do relate to estate cars, Range Rovers etc. Be aware there are a host of adjustments which can be made to the tax payable. These include adjustments for the number of days cars were available for private use, shared cars, pool cars, disabled drivers etc.

Employers' Responsibilities

Class 1A contributions are paid annually in arrears. Contributions are due on 19 July each year. Contributions should be added to the June national insurance calculation (which is also due on 19 July). This means that the 1997/98 payment is due on 19 July 1998.

The regulations require the employer to enter the Class 1A contributions on the P11 deductions working sheet and the P14 annual certificate (using Table Y). The employer should also complete form P35 for the year in which the contribution is paid. For example, the 1997/98 payments are recorded on the P14 and P35 for 1998/99.

When an employee with a company car leaves during the year, the employer is required to create a P11 for the following year. This will record the Class 1A contribution. For example, if an employee leaves during 1997/98, a P11 must be created for 1998/99 to reflect the payment in July 1998. Include the payment on the 1998/99 P35.

Check Social Security booklet CA33 (also called Manual 4 – Cars and Fuel) for full details.

Exercise 11

How much Class 1A contribution would an employer have to pay for an employee who had the following car during the 1998/1999 tax year.

- a five year old car
- original price £11,250
- engine capacity 1800cc
- driven by petrol
- covering 26,000 miles per annum.

Check your answer with page 165.

Class 2 Contributions

These are paid by self employed persons at a weekly flat rate. Persons are liable to Class 2 contributions if they are:

- normally self-employed *and*
- 16 or over *and*
- under pension age *and*
- have not been exempted from liability.

If earnings from self employment are expected to be less than the 'exemption limit', you can apply for exemption for that year. From 6 April 1998, the flat rate is £6.35 per week and the small earnings exemption is £3,590 per annum. The exemption limit usually changes each year in the budget. You can arrange to pay Class 2 contributions in one of two ways:

Direct Debit

You may pay national insurance contributions monthly by direct debit through your bank or National Girobank account. Contributions will not be debited for any complete weeks you prove that you could not work because of illness.

Quarterly Billing System

From 11 April 1993, self employed persons have had another way to pay Class 2 national insurance contributions. They will be billed, by the DSS, quarterly in arrears during the months of July, October, January and April. This system replaces the contribution card method which formally lapsed on 10 April 1993. See Department of Social Security leaflet CA05 for full details.

Class 2 contributions count for the following benefits:

- basic sickness benefit
- basic invalidity benefit
- basic retirement pension
- basic widow's benefit
- basic maternity allowance
- child's special allowance
- death grant
- income support.

Class 2 contributions do not count for:

- unemployment benefit
- additional earnings related pension
- additional earnings related widow's benefit
- industrial injuries benefits.

Class 3 Contributions

Class 3 contributions are for those who do not make contributions via their work. They are voluntary contributions designed to preserve people's entitlement to benefits.

Class 3 contributions are paid at a **flat rate**. From April 1998, this rate is £6.25 per week. Collection is via the quarterly billing system.

Class 4 Contributions

If your profits from self employment are over a certain limit, you have to pay Class 4 contributions. These are in addition to Class 2 contributions. Class 4 contributions are earnings related. There is a lower limit for liability below which no Class 4 contribution is payable. The lower annual limit from 6 April 1998 is £7,310. There is also an upper limit which was set at £25,220 from the same date. No contributions are payable on earnings above the upper limit. Between these limits, tax is levied at a fixed rate of 6% of profits. The profits assessed for Class 4 differ slightly from those assessed for Schedule D Cases I and II income tax.

For example, no deductions are allowable for:

- trade charges (eg patent royalties)

- certain interest charges. (However, interest paid by a partner personally on a loan used to provide partnership capital does reduce the Class 4 chargeable profit.)

Between tax years 1985/86 and 1995/96, a self employed person was able to reclaim 50% of the Class 4 contributions as a deduction from total taxable profit in that tax year. This relief was abolished commencing with the 1996/97 tax year.

Class 4 is a profit tax

Payments of Class 4 NIC

- Class 4 contributions are collected by the Inland Revenue along with related income tax. Half is payable on 1 January in the year of assessment and half on 1 July following the year of assessment.

- Both a husband and wife can be liable to Class 4 contributions.

  Where a husband and wife are in partnership, separate Class 4 contributions are assessed on the wife's and husband's share of the profit.

Example 12 Mr Martin Class 4 Contributions

We shall assume: that the lower limit is   £7,310
                    that the upper limit is   £25,220
                    that the rate of contribution is 6%

For the year in question, Mr Martin made self employed profits of £13,200. Using the rates shown above, calculate his liability to Class 4.

How much income tax relief would his Class 4 contribution attract?

	£
Net profit	13200
Less lower liability	7310
Amount liable	5890

£5890 x 6%   £353.40

Undertake the following exercise.

Exercise 12

Using the same rates and limits, calculate Susan's Class 4 liability. The profit made was £29,000.

Net profit

Upper limit for Class 4
Less lower limit for Class 4

Amount of profit liable   £

Liability £ _____ x _____ % = £

Compare your answer with the model on page 167.

If you Have More than One Job

If you work for an employer as well as being self employed, you will have to pay Class 1 contributions as well as Class 2. If your earnings from self employment are high enough, you will also have to pay Class 4 contributions.

BUT there is an upper limit to the amount of contributions you have to pay in any tax year and, if your total contributions are more than this, the excess will normally be refunded to you.

Tax Hint: If the above applies to you, claim deferment from Class 2 and Class 4 contributions on DSS leaflet NP18. Liability on Class 2 and 4 will then be assessed when total Class 1 earnings are known, which is after the tax year ends.

Do I Have all the Right Manuals, Tables, etc?

You should have:

- *Employer's Quick Guide to PAYE and NICs CWG1 April 1998*

- *Employer's Further Guide to PAYE and NICs CWG2 (1998)*

- *National Insurance Not Contracted Out Contributions Tables CA38 from April 1998*
  (You will only be given a copy of National Insurance Contracted Out Tables CA39 if your employees belong to an approved pension scheme)

- *Statutory Sick Pay and Statutory Maternity Pay Tables CA35/36 from April 1998.*

- *Manual 4 – Cars and Fuel Manual for Employers CA33*

- *National Insurance for Company Directors CA44.*

Need More Help?

Call the Social Security Advice Line for Employers on 0345 143 143, or call the Contribution Agency at your local Social Security office.

Chapter 6

Corporation Tax

We saw in Chapter 2 that individuals and partnerships pay tax under Schedule D. We will now see how companies are taxed. Up until 1965 companies paid income tax on their profits just like sole traders and partnerships. After 1965 companies became liable to corporation tax. Although corporation tax is different to income tax, there are many similarities. In fact corporation tax is broadly based on the rules of Schedule D Case I (which we looked at when we were examining self-employment).

What is a Company?

A company comprises a group of people who join together to conduct a business. A company is owned by its shareholders and managed by its employees. Legal responsibility for the running of the company lies with the company directors who are also employees of the company. Companies are often known as 'limited' companies, this is because the liabilities of the company belong to the company and not to directors or shareholders (providing they have acted in accordance with

Employees can be shareholders

the laws governing companies). Shareholders can be employees. Unlike a partnership, a company has a separate legal entity. For example, it can enter into contracts, sue and be sued. A company has to pay taxes on its profits, these taxes are collected under the rules of corporation tax.

Who Pays Corporation Tax?

Companies which are resident in the UK pay corporation tax on their profits wherever those profits arise. Foreign owned companies which have branches located in the UK also pay corporation tax on their UK earnings. Corporation tax also applies to unincorporated bodies like building societies, insurance companies, clubs and associations, and government owned bodies like the Bank of England.

Corporation tax does not apply to bodies such as approved pension schemes, local authorities and Crown Agencies.

Sports clubs pay corporation tax!

What is Corporation Tax?

Corporation tax is a tax based on 'chargeable' profits. Chargeable profits comprise:

- Trading Profits
- Capital Gains
- Investment Income.

Trading Profits

In broad outline, trading profits are calculated along the same lines as sole traders and partnerships. Many of the rules relating to the profit calculation are regulated by the Schedule system of taxation outlined earlier in Chapter 2. The distinction between allowable and non-allowable expenses apply in the same way as we have already seen earlier. If a company has income from property then the taxable profit is decided according to the rules of Schedule A. Although a company is a separate legal entity, it is not a 'person' in the sense that it is entitled to personal tax allowances. It can never earn income under the rules of Schedule E since the company cannot become an 'employee' in the true sense of the word.

Capital Gains

Capital gains are calculated along the same broad lines as Capital Gains Tax (CGT) as it relates to individuals. However, the company is not entitled to the annual CGT exemption (currently £6,800) because a company is not an individual. A capital gain can only exist once the gain is crystallised. In general assets can increase in value without incurring tax. It is only when the asset is sold and the gain is realised that the gain becomes taxable.

Investment Income

It is common for companies to receive interest on deposited funds. If the interest has not been taxed at source it is assessed under Schedule D Case III. If the interest has been taxed at source, eg building society interest, then the net receipt is grossed up and then charged to corporation tax. Where tax has been deducted at source the tax credit is available to reduce the overall liability of the company. Building societies can pay interest to companies on a gross basis.

Companies can receive rental income

Many companies own property and land on which they receive income. This income is calculated using the rules of Schedule A. The net profit is charged to corporation tax.

Adjusting the Profit for Corporation Tax

In the chapter on self-employment we looked at the adjustments to the accounting profit necessary to arrive at the taxable profit. You may remember that non allowable items were added to profit in the profit and loss account. Income not derived from trading was deducted from the profit and loss account. The same adjustments are made to companies accounts when deriving the profit chargeable to corporation tax. Let us look at a profit and loss account for a company. We will make some adjustments for tax purposes:

Adjusting the profit!

The company has the following profit and loss account for the year ended 31 March 1997.

	£	£
Sales		345720
Cost Of Sales (Note i)		(134540)
Gross Profit		211,180
Expenses		
Administration Costs (Note ii)	64590	
Distribution	32760	
Marketing	18092	
Financial (Note iii)	23458	
		(138900)
		72280
Non Trading Income (Note iv)		5635
Profit before tax		77915
Corporation Tax		(28526)
Profit after tax		49389
Dividends Paid		(6000)
Retained profits for the year		43389

Notes:

(i) Cost of Sales includes £42,680 depreciation
(ii) Administration costs include legal expenses of £2,000 for acquisition of a lease plus Stamp duty of £900
(iii) Financial costs include a donation of £1,000
(iv) The non trading income relates to profit on sale of assets

The adjustment of profit for corporation tax purposes would look as follows:

	£	£
Retained Profit per accounts		43389
Add Back:		
Depreciation (Note v)	42680	
Legal expenses (Note vi)	2000	
Stamp duty (Note vii)	900	
Donation (Note viii)	1000	
Corporation tax (Note ix)	28525	
Dividends (Note x)	6000	
		81105
		124494
Less profit on sale of assets (Note xi)		(5635)
Schedule D Case I profit		118859

Corporation tax due £118,859 x 24% = £28,526.16 (assuming a 24% corp tax rate)

Notes continued:

(v)   Depreciation is added back, capital allowances will be claimed instead (see note below).

(vi)   Legal costs relate to acquisition of a lease which is a capital item; this is not allowable in the profit and loss account. It will be a capital addition within the balance sheet.

(vii) Stamp duty is capital expenditure.

(viii) Donations are generally not allowable.

(ix)   The dividends of £6,000 and corporation tax of £28,526 are *applications* of profit and are, therefore, not allowable. We could have commenced the computation before deducting these items, ie £77,915 and, indeed, this is the normal method.

(x)   The profit on the sales of assets is not a taxable receipt. It is taken into account within the capital allowance computation.

Accounting Periods

The amount of corporation tax payable depends on two periods, these are:

- the accounting year end date for the company
- the government's corporation tax year.

The tax year for corporation tax runs from 1 April one year to 31 March in the following year. Therefore the 1998 corporation tax year runs from 1 April 1998 to 31 March 1999. The corporation tax year is termed the 'financial year'. Note that this is different from the income tax year which runs from 6 April one year to 5 April the following year.

A company is free to opt for any accounting year end it chooses. Sometimes companies will choose the same year end as the tax year end, ie 31 March. Often, however, the company's accounting year end will be different from the tax year end. When this happens, the profit is apportioned between the tax years. If the tax rates are the same in successive tax years appointing the profit between years will not effect the tax paid. However, if the tax rates change from one year to the next, the profit will be taxed at two different rates. Here is an example.

Example 10

Suppose that a company's accounting year end date was 30 September 1997 and the taxable profit was £100,000. Further suppose that the following corporation tax rates were in force:

Corporation rate   1 April 1996 – 31 March 1997   24% (Financial year 1996)
Corporation rate   1 April 1997 – 31 March 1998   21% (Financial year 1997)

There is no need to produce separate accounts for each tax year. You simply apportion the business profit according to the number of days falling within each tax year. In our case there were 365 days in the trading year between 1 October 1996 and 30 September 1997.

There are 182 days between 1 October 1996 and 31 March 1997. These 182 days fall within the financial year 1996 where they are taxed at 24%.

There are 183 days between 1 April 1997 and 30 September 1997. These 183 days fall within the financial year 1997 where they are taxed at 21%

The tax calculation would therefore look as follows:

Financial Year 1996	£100,000 x 182/365	=	£49863
Financial Year 1997	£100,000 x 183/365	=	£50137
	Total	=	£100000

Corporation Tax due:

Financial Year 1996	£49,863 x 24%	=	£11967.12
Financial Year 1997	£50,137 x 21%	=	£10528.77
Total Corporation Tax due		=	£22495.89

Exercise 13

Z Ltd has an accounting year ending 31 December 1997. The total profit chargeable to corporation tax was £124,000. Calculate the corporation tax payable by Z Ltd

The rate of tax for the financial year 1996 was 24%
The rate of tax for the financial year 1997 was 21%

Check your answer with page 167.

Occasionally, a company's accounting 'year' will exceed 12 months. If this happens, the accounts must be split so that each accounting period is 12 months or less. For corporation tax purposes, the accounting period assessed for corporation tax can never exceed 12 months.

What are the Rates of Tax?

There are two main rates of corporation tax. For example, for the tax year commencing 1 April 1998, these were:

Full rate	31%
Small companies rate	21%

To be eligible for the small companies rate, the company's profits must be below £300,000. Companies with profits exceeding £1,500,000 are charged at the full rate. What happens to company profits between £300,000 and £1,500,000?

Between the upper limit of £1,500,000 and lower limit of £300,000, tax is charged at the full rate, **but** the amount of tax paid is reduced by an amount called the 'marginal relief'. Marginal relief is calculated from the following formula.

Big companies pay corporation tax at 31%

$$(M - P) \times \frac{I}{P} \times F$$

This is what the letters stand for.

M – the upper maximum (currently £1.5 million)

F – small companies marginal relief fraction (for the tax year commencing 1 April 1998 the marginal relief fraction was 1/40).

I – chargeable profit. These are trading profits plus capital gains arising during the trading year. They are also known as 'basic profits'.

P – these are chargeable profits **plus** any UK dividends which have been received with tax credits attached. This is also called 'total profits'.

The formula could be rewritten as:

Marginal Fraction x (Upper Limit - Total Profits) x $\dfrac{\text{Basic Profits}}{\text{Total Profits}}$

Example 11

A company had £1,000,000 of chargeable profits (basic profits). It also had £100,000 of UK dividends. This means that total profit was £1,100,000. How much corporation tax should it pay?

		£
Corporation tax (31%) at full rate on £1,000,000 (basic profits)		310000
less Marginal relief $\dfrac{1}{40}$ x (£1,500,000 – £1,100,000) x $\dfrac{1,000,000}{1,100,000}$		9090
Corporation Tax payable		300910

Therefore the marginal rate of tax is approximately 30%, ie:

$$\frac{\text{Tax due}}{\text{Basic profits}} = \frac{300910}{1000000} = 30\%$$

When do Companies Pay their Corporation Tax?

A revised method of payment for corporation tax was introduced on 1 October 1993. This method is called 'pay and file'. As suggested by its name, the company first *pays* the tax due on profits and then *files* a return with the Inland Revenue later. The tax payment must be made within nine months after the company's year end. The return and accounts must be filed within 12 months of the company's year end.

In most cases the company manages to complete its accounts within nine months. It is then able to calculate its corporation tax liability. However, if the company is not able to prepare its accounts within nine months, it must estimate the tax due and make a payment within the nine month period. When the tax liability is finally agreed with the Inland Revenue any underestimation of its liability must be paid with interest. If the company has overestimated its liability it will be due a repayment with interest.

The corporation tax return is made on form CT200. This requests details of the accounting periods, profit or losses, any claim to capital allowances, any claim for reliefs by the company, and a computation of the corporation tax liability. A copy of the annual accounts must be submitted with the return. If a return is delivered late the following penalties apply:

Delay From Due Date	Penalty	
0 – 3 Months	£100	(+ £500 if this is the third consecutive late return)
3 – 6 Months	£200	(+ £1000 if this is the third consecutive late return)
6 – 12 Months	£200 + 10% of unpaid tax	
12 + Months	£200 + 20% of unpaid tax	

Dividends and Advance Corporation Tax

A company will normally reward its shareholders by paying them a dividend once or twice a year. When a company pays a dividend, it must withhold from the shareholders an amount of tax called Advance Corporation Tax (ACT). The rate of ACT is set annually by the government. For the current year (1998), the rate of ACT is one quarter of the **net** dividend paid to shareholders. For example, suppose a shareholder was due a **net** dividend of £80, a tax credit would be added of £20, giving a gross dividend of £100. The ACT deducted equates to 25% of the **net** dividend. In this case, the amount of ACT payable would be a quarter of the amount actually distributed, ie a quarter of £80 which is £20.

The company pays the ACT collected to the government under a quarterly return system. The normal quarterly return dates are 31 March, 30 June, 30 September and 31 December. The ACT collected during any quarter must be paid to the Collector of Taxes within 14 days of the end of that quarter. There is one exception to this rule, a quarter will terminate earlier if the company's accounting year end falls between two quarterly return dates. When this happens any ACT due is payable 14 days after the end of the accounting year, not at the end of the reporting quarter.

The ACT is paid to the Collector of Taxes, it counts as a part payment of corporation tax for that company.

Example 12

T Ltd has a profit chargeable to corporation tax of £75,000 for its accounting year ended 31 March 1998. Assume that the rate of corporation tax is 21%. The total corporation tax charge would be:

$$£75,000 \times 21\% = £15,750$$

This is the 'mainstream' corporation tax liability.

However, if a **net** dividend of £28,760 was paid out on 31 October 1997 then the ACT would be:

$$£28,760 \times 1/4 = £7,190 \text{ (payable by 14 January 1998)}$$

This means that the company would owe the balance of the corporation tax payable which is:

	Mainstream liability	£15750
less	ACT	£7190
		£8560

The mainstream liability has been reduced by the ACT paid on 14 January 1998. The balance of the tax due (£8,560) should be paid by 1 October 1998.

Exercise 14

Work out the ACT due on the following net dividends and state the due date for payment of the ACT. The company accounting year ends on 30/11/98.

  1)   Net dividend of £187, paid 28/2/98
  2)   Net dividend of £246, paid 30/8/98
  3)   Net dividend of £292, paid 31/10/98

Check your answer with page 168.

If a company has surplus ACT, it can be carried back to accounting periods beginning six years before the accounting period in which the surplus ACT arose. The ACT must be applied to the most recent periods first. If there are no periods to carry back ACT to (because for example the company previously made losses or it is a new company) the ACT may be carried forward and used against future years profit.

ACT will be abolished from 6 April 1999. This means that payment of a dividend will no longer be followed by an ACT payment. However companies whose annual taxable profits are in excess of £1,500,000 will in future have to pay corporation tax in four quarterly instalments.

Losses

The treatment of losses for corporation tax purposes is a complicated subject which cannot be dealt with in detail in this book. If your company makes a loss you should take advice on the treatment of the loss for corporate tax purposes.

In general terms if a loss is incurred by a company, it is possible to use the loss to reduce current, future or past corporation tax. The following points summarise the main ways in which losses can be used. In the following notes ICTA 1998 is an abbreviation for the Income and Corporate Taxes Act 1998. This is the main body of statute law for taxation.

- A trading loss can be used to offset profits arising in the same trading period. For example a company could make a loss on its trading operations and a capital gain on the sale of its assets. The trading loss can be used to recover the tax due on the capital gain. (Section 393A(1)(a) ICTA 1998)

- A trading loss can be carried forward and utilised against future profits reducing the corporation tax payable in the future. (Section 393 ICTA 1998)

- Losses occurring after 1 July 1997 may be carried back to the 12 month period prior to that in which the loss was incurred. (Section 393 A (1)(b) ICTA 1998)

Self Assessment for Companies

We mentioned in an earlier chapter that self assessment for individuals commenced on 6 April 1997. In future, Corporation taxes will also be subject to self assessment. Corporation tax self assessment will be introduced for accounting periods ending on or after 1 July 1999. Any company commencing a 12 month accounting period on or after 2 July 1998 will come under the self assessment provisions.

Self assessment for companies will be relatively straightforward. To a large part companies already self assess their corporate tax liability when they complete the annual return form CT200. This contains a calculation of the amount of corporate tax payable. This form will become more detailed in future.

Self Assessment!

The effect of this change is to transfer responsibility for the assessment of corporation tax from the Inland Revenue to the company. At present the company submits form CT200 together with its accounts and the Inland Revenue issue an assessment. Under self assessment the Inland Revenue will no longer issue assessments. The company must self assess its liability and pay the tax to the Inland Revenue.

Chapter 7

Styles of Trading

So far we have looked at sole traders, partnerships and limited liability companies. The following paragraphs give you more background information on each style of trading including notes on taxation and legal issues.

These notes cannot tell you everything there is to know about the topic. This is an area where paying for professional advice could be the cheapest option in the long run. At the end of the day, only you can decide which option suits you. You have to weigh up the conflicting pressures of tax, financial exposure, administrative convenience etc implicit in each option.

Sole Trader

A sole trader is a person who owns a business, irrespective of its size. Legally, there is no division between the business and the proprietor.

There are few government controls. For example, there is usually no legal necessity to have accounts audited. There are no particular formalities required. If the proprietor wishes to discontinue a business (provided it is solvent), he is free to do so.

A Sole Trader!

Sole traders face one major worry. They are personally liable for all of the debts of the business. Personal assets like home, cars and furniture could be lost if the business fails to meet its debts. The main points for a sole trader are summarised below.

The trader:

- Is self employed and is not recognised in law as a separate entity for business purposes. He/she is taxed under Schedule D.

- Carries all responsibility for running the business.

- Takes all the profit of the business. Funds can be withdrawn from the business at will.

- Is liable for all debts of the business.

- Can lose personal possessions and be made bankrupt for any debts of the business.

- Can be sued and can sue other persons (or organisations) for debts owed.

- Is not regulated by any specific law but must comply with all national and local laws.

- Does not have to register the business with any government office or department apart from those listed below.

- Must register the business with the Inland Revenue for taxation purposes and the Department of Social Security for national insurance purposes.

- May be required to register for VAT depending on the level of turnover.

- Can prepare and submit his own accounts to the Inland Revenue if he so wishes.

- Must run the business with a view to making a profit. This does not preclude some losses but the intention to make a profit must exist otherwise the Inland Revenue would not consider it to be a commercial venture.

Advantages of Trading as a Sole Trader

- little formality
- generally lower accounting charges
- no need to publish profits
- proprietors taxed under Schedule D – slightly more flexible
- national insurance cheaper for sole traders than directors
- pension contributions easy and flexible.

Disadvantages of Trading as a Sole Trader

- full personal liability for debts of the business
- raising new capital is probably more difficult.

Partnership

Partnerships consist of two or more persons running a business with the intention of making and sharing profits. Losses need not be shared in the same proportions as profits.

Partners!

The debts of a partnership fall jointly and severally on the partners. This means that one partner could be held liable for all of the debts of the partnership. This could occur, for example, with the Inland Revenue. Normally, each partner settles his/her tax liability individually with the Inland Revenue. However, if one or more partners were unable (or unwilling) to pay their share of the tax, then the Inland Revenue is free to recover tax from *any* partner who they believe is able to pay. Of course the partner paying the debts of other partners is then open to sue the other partners for their share of the liability.

Each member of a partnership is effectively a self-employed individual, so all of the comments regarding sole traders apply. All partners act as agents for each other. The act of one partner in the name of the partnership is binding on all other parties.

No formal partnership agreement is necessary but it is highly recommended and should cover the following 'heads of agreement':

- Amounts of capital to be contributed to the partnership by each partner.

- How profits and losses are to be divided among the partners.

- The duties and functions of the partners.

- What happens on the death of a partner.

- Partners' responsibilities for debts incurred by the partnership.

- How assets are to be valued on changes in partnership.

- What happens if someone joins, leaves or retires from the partnership. What obligations does the person joining or leaving have to the other partners.

- In the absence of any formal partnership agreement, the Partnership Act of 1890 will apply.

Advantages of Trading as a Partnership

- shared responsibility
- additional capital availability
- cover for illness, holidays etc
- greater range of skills available
- no requirement to publish the accounts.

Disadvantages of Trading as a Partnership

- unlimited liability
- a new partnership is formed when anyone joins or leaves
- disputes between members can be troublesome. Someone once said that 'a leakier ship did never put to sea'.

Limited Companies

A company is an association of people who join together to conduct a business. Limited companies are more tightly controlled than sole traders or partnerships. Their activities are regulated by various Company Acts.

A limited company begins life when two or more people subscribe for shares in a business. Small limited companies are normally formed with 100 £1 ordinary shares. For example, Mr and Mrs Brown could subscribe for 100 ordinary £1 shares in the company. They will have 50 ordinary £1 shares each and pay the company £50 each for these shares. They are known as shareholders. The shareholders own the business.

Every company must have directors. Directors are employees of the company. They are paid wages like any other employee. So, if Mr and Mrs Brown run the company, they will be both shareholders and employees at the same time. Every company needs to have a Company Secretary, normally one of the directors will fill this role.

If you wish to start a small limited company, you will usually buy one 'off the shelf' from a company formation agent. Formation agents are businesses which specialise in selling 'new' companies. Your accountant or solicitor will normally make this purchase for you. On formation you will receive:

- A Certificate of Incorporation
- A copy of the Memorandum and Articles of Association
- Share Certificates
- Company Seal
- A Company Register.

The Memorandum states, amongst other things, the name and address of the company, its objects, and the amount of share capital with which it is registered.

The Articles of Association set down the regulations governing the internal affairs of the company. They cover such matters as the appointment and proceedings of directors, restrictions on the issue and transfer of shares etc.

Both the Articles of Association and the Memorandum of Association need to be registered under the Companies Act. Once accepted, the Registrar of Companies will issue a Certificate of Incorporation which will bring the company into existence.
On receipt of the Certificate of Incorporation, the company will acquire a company seal which will be used to emboss any additional documents. The company then issues share certificates to its owners. At this juncture, the company can commence trading.

Once trading, the company becomes subject to the Companies Acts. These place certain duties on the company such as:

- The company will need to keep proper books and records. It will have to employ a qualified accountant to prepare and audit its accounts. A qualified accountant is, for example, a chartered accountant who is also a registered auditor. Under company law, the company is required to submit its books and records for audit annually. This means your accountant will examine these books and records in some considerable detail. He will check that the company's accounts conform to his institute's standards. If satisfied, he will certify that the company has complied with company law.

- Directors meetings held during the year must be minuted.

- The company has to pay corporation tax on its profits.

- The company has to make annual returns to the Registrar of Companies.

- The company needs to send a set of accounts to the Registrar of Companies. The company needs to pay a filing fee (£32 at the time of writing) to the Registrar of Companies.

- The company needs to hold an Annual General Meeting (AGM) of shareholders.

Most limited companies need an audit

We have only briefly touched on this subject. As you can see, forming and running a company can be time consuming.

Be sure to take proper advice if you are thinking of incorporating your business. There are many taxation implications to forming a limited company that lie beyond the scope of this book. It is essential that you are satisfied that the best structure for your business is a limited company. Once you have incorporated the business, it can be difficult to disincorporate or wind up the company. Take professional advice *before* deciding under which heading you wish to trade.

The shareholders of a limited company cannot use the assets of a company for their own personal use, nor can they withdraw funds from the company at will. Indeed, it is illegal for the company to make loans to directors in most instances.

Most of the benefits that are provided to directors (or their families) are taxable, usually on the basis of the cost to the limited company.

Advantages of Trading as a Limited Liability Company

The main advantage of a limited company arises because the company has a separate legal entity from its members. Normally, members have no further liability for the debts incurred by the business once they have subscribed for their shares. However, the protection of limited liability for the company's debts may not *necessarily* provide members with complete protection. If a director knowingly incurs debts on behalf of the company, when he knows the company will not be able to pay, then the director can be sued for wrongful or fraudulent trading (which may also lead to his/her disqualification).

If a company goes into liquidation and there is evidence of fraudulent trading, the director could be ordered to contribute to the company's assets personally.

Other advantages of a limited company include continuity. The company acts in perpetual succession until it is wound up. Therefore, changes in shareholders do not affect the continuity of the trading activities of the company. It may be possible to distinguish separately the management of the company from its ownership.

Companies accounts are filed with the Registrar of Companies at Companies House. They are open to inspection by third parties. This is why some trade suppliers and creditors may deal more readily with companies than with individuals or partnerships. One major advantage of a company is that it can provide security for its borrowings by means of a 'floating charge' on its assets. This option is not available to the sole trader.

Disadvantages of Trading as a Limited Liability Company

One of the major disadvantages of a company is the requirement for compliance under the Companies Acts. This can often involve some expense. The necessity for a formal audit of the company's records was relaxed for small companies in the Finance Act 1994. Under these provisions, the requirement for a statutory audit has been removed for companies with annual turnovers of less than £90,000. An independent accountant's report is required for companies with an annual turnover of between £90,000 and £350,000. These measures will reduce costs for small companies. But, because of the need to comply with all of the Companies Act, company running costs will always be higher than sole traders or partnerships.

Banks and other creditors often require the company directors to personally guarantee any loans advanced to the company. This is particularly common in the early years of a company's trading. In the event of the company failing, the bankers and creditors would seek to enforce the personal guarantees. This results in the debt of the company being transferred to the directors personally, up to the value of their guarantees.

Audit Fees

Your accountant has to undertake strict audit procedures, this results in greater accountancy fees than those for sole traders or partnerships. Sole traders' accounts normally run to two pages. Even a small company will be lucky to get away with eight pages of accounts. These normally consist of:

- page showing details of directors, secretary, registered office, bankers, auditors and company number

- directors report

- auditors report

- summarised profit and loss account

- balance sheet

- notes to accounts - possibly two to three pages

- trading and profit and loss accounts

- directors accounts.

In addition, abbreviated accounts are required for submission to the Registrar of Companies.

Summary

☐ A limited company is recognised in law as a separate legal entity.

☐ A company can be sued and can sue other persons or organisations.

☐ A company can own property, goods and equipment.

☐ A company can employ people. Remember directors are also employees.

☐ A company must hold an annual general meeting of its shareholders.

☐ A company can vote dividends to its shareholders.

☐ A company must have accounts audited by a qualified and independent person. However, remember there are relaxations for small companies.

☐ A company must pay corporation tax on its profits (under the 'pay and file' system).

☐ A company must make annual returns to the Registrar of Companies.

☐ The company and its directors must conform to all laws detailed in the Companies Acts.

Tax Publications Guide

Inland Revenue

P6   Code notification from tax office

P9(T)   Code notification from tax office for use in next tax year

P11   Deductions working sheet
P11(D)   Return of employees' expenses payments & benefits paid during tax year

P14   Individual end of year summary of pay, tax, NIC and SSP/SMP

P30B   Payslips for sending with payments to the Accounts Office
P30BC   Payslip booklet containing payslips

P31   For use by a new employer who wishes to pay quarterly

P32   For keeping monthly totals of tax, NIC, SSP/SMP

P34   For ordering fresh supplies of forms from your tax office

P35   Employer's annual return

P38   Employer's supplementary return for employees who were not entered on
P38A   form P35

P38S   For use by students to claim special treatment when employed during
            holidays

P45   For use where an employee leaves a job and when an employee starts a job

P46   For use when a new employee does not produce a P45

P46(Car)   Advance details of car/fuel provided for employee

P60   Certificate of employee's pay and tax deducted. This can be either a separate form or the third part of form P14

IR56   Leaflet giving guidance on who is employed or self-employed

Tables A   Pay Adjustment Tables

Tables   Taxable Pay Tables
LR+B-D

DSS Contributions Agency

Employer's Quick Guide to PAYE and NICs CWG1 April 1998

Employer's Further Guide to PAYE and NICs CWG2 (1998)

National Insurance Not Contracted Out Contributions Tables CA38 from April 1998

Statutory Sick Pay and Statutory Maternity Pay Tables CA35/36 from April 1998

Manual 4 – Cars and Fuel Manual for Employers CA33

National Insurance for Company Directors CA44.

HM Customs and Excise VAT Publications

Leaflet No	Title
700/1/92	*Should I be Registered for VAT?*
700/11/93	*Cancelling Your Registration?*
700/12/93	*Filling in Your VAT Return*
700/13/94	*VAT Publications*
700/15/91	*The Ins and Outs of VAT*
700/18/91	*Relief from VAT on Bad Debts*
700/21/91	*Keeping Records and Accounts*
700/26/92	*Visits by VAT Officers*
700/34/88	*Supplies of Staff, Including Directors and Other Office Holders*
700/35/88	*Business Gifts*
700/41/88	*Late Registration: Penalties and Reasonable Excuse*
700/42/93	*Misdeclaration Penalty*
700/43/93	*Interest*
700/45/93	*How to Correct Errors You Find on Your VAT Returns*
706/1/92	*Self Supply of Stationery*
727/7/93 – 727/15/93	*Retail Schemes*

Notice No	Title	Date
700	*The VAT Guide*	March 1996
727	*Retail Schemes*	April 1993
731	*Cash Accounting*	May 1994
732	*Annual Accounting*	January 1996

Sample Tax and NI Tables

Month 1

TABLE A - PAY ADJUSTMENT

Apr 6 to May 5

Code	Total pay adjustment to date (£)	Code	Total pay adjustment to date (£)	Code	Total pay adjustment to date (£)	Code	Total pay adjustment to date (£)	Code	Total pay adjustment to date (£)	Code	Total pay adjustment to date (£)	Code	Total pay adjustment to date (£)	Code	Total pay adjustment to date (£)	Code	Total pay adjustment to date (£)
0	NIL																
1	1.59	61	51.59	121	101.59	181	151.59	241	201.59	301	251.59	351	293.25	401	334.92	451	376.59
2	2.42	62	52.42	122	102.42	182	152.42	242	202.42	302	252.42	352	294.09	402	335.75	452	377.42
3	3.25	63	53.25	123	103.25	183	153.25	243	203.25	303	253.25	353	294.92	403	336.59	453	378.25
4	4.09	64	54.09	124	104.09	184	154.09	244	204.09	304	254.09	354	295.75	404	337.42	454	379.09
5	4.92	65	54.92	125	104.92	185	154.92	245	204.92	305	254.92	355	296.59	405	338.25	455	379.92
6	5.75	66	55.75	126	105.75	186	155.75	246	205.75	306	255.75	356	297.42	406	339.09	456	380.75
7	6.59	67	56.59	127	106.59	187	156.59	247	206.59	307	256.59	357	298.25	407	339.92	457	381.59
8	7.42	68	57.42	128	107.42	188	157.42	248	207.42	308	257.42	358	299.09	408	340.75	458	382.42
9	8.25	69	58.25	129	108.25	189	158.25	249	208.25	309	258.25	359	299.92	409	341.59	459	383.25
10	9.09	70	59.09	130	109.09	190	159.09	250	209.09	310	259.09	360	300.75	410	342.42	460	384.09
11	9.92	71	59.92	131	109.92	191	159.92	251	209.92	311	259.92	361	301.59	411	343.25	461	384.92
12	10.75	72	60.75	132	110.75	192	160.75	252	210.75	312	260.75	362	302.42	412	344.09	462	385.75
13	11.59	73	61.59	133	111.59	193	161.59	253	211.59	313	261.59	363	303.25	413	344.92	463	386.59
14	12.42	74	62.42	134	112.42	194	162.42	254	212.42	314	262.42	364	304.09	414	345.75	464	387.42
15	13.25	75	63.25	135	113.25	195	163.25	255	213.25	315	263.25	365	304.92	415	346.59	465	388.25
16	14.09	76	64.09	136	114.09	196	164.09	256	214.09	316	264.09	366	305.75	416	347.42	466	389.09
17	14.92	77	64.92	137	114.92	197	164.92	257	214.92	317	264.92	367	306.59	417	348.25	467	389.92
18	15.75	78	65.75	138	115.75	198	165.75	258	215.75	318	265.75	368	307.42	418	349.09	468	390.75
19	16.59	79	66.59	139	116.59	199	166.59	259	216.59	319	266.59	369	308.25	419	349.92	469	391.59
20	17.42	80	67.42	140	117.42	200	167.42	260	217.42	320	267.42	370	309.09	420	350.75	470	392.42
21	18.25	81	68.25	141	118.25	201	168.25	261	218.25	321	268.25	371	309.92	421	351.59	471	393.25
22	19.09	82	69.09	142	119.09	202	169.09	262	219.09	322	269.09	372	310.75	422	352.42	472	394.09
23	19.92	83	69.92	143	119.92	203	169.92	263	219.92	323	269.92	373	311.59	423	353.25	473	394.92
24	20.75	84	70.75	144	120.75	204	170.75	264	220.75	324	270.75	374	312.42	424	354.09	474	395.75
25	21.59	85	71.59	145	121.59	205	171.59	265	221.59	325	271.59	375	313.25	425	354.92	475	396.59
26	22.42	86	72.42	146	122.42	206	172.42	266	222.42	326	272.42	376	314.09	426	355.75	476	397.42
27	23.25	87	73.25	147	123.25	207	173.25	267	223.25	327	273.25	377	314.92	427	356.59	477	398.25
28	24.09	88	74.09	148	124.09	208	174.09	268	224.09	328	274.09	378	315.75	428	357.42	478	399.09
29	24.92	89	74.92	149	124.92	209	174.92	269	224.92	329	274.92	379	316.59	429	358.25	479	399.92
30	25.75	90	75.75	150	125.75	210	175.75	270	225.75	330	275.75	380	317.42	430	359.09	480	400.75
31	26.59	91	76.59	151	126.59	211	176.59	271	226.59	331	276.59	381	318.25	431	359.92	481	401.59
32	27.42	92	77.42	152	127.42	212	177.42	272	227.42	332	277.42	382	319.09	432	360.75	482	402.42
33	28.25	93	78.25	153	128.25	213	178.25	273	228.25	333	278.25	383	319.92	433	361.59	483	403.25
34	29.09	94	79.09	154	129.09	214	179.09	274	229.09	334	279.09	384	320.75	434	362.42	484	404.09
35	29.92	95	79.92	155	129.92	215	179.92	275	229.92	335	279.92	385	321.59	435	363.25	485	404.92
36	30.75	96	80.75	156	130.75	216	180.75	276	230.75	336	280.75	386	322.42	436	364.09	486	405.75
37	31.59	97	81.59	157	131.59	217	181.59	277	231.59	337	281.59	387	323.25	437	364.92	487	406.59
38	32.42	98	82.42	158	132.42	218	182.42	278	232.42	338	282.42	388	324.09	438	365.75	488	407.42
39	33.25	99	83.25	159	133.25	219	183.25	279	233.25	339	283.25	389	324.92	439	366.59	489	408.25
40	34.09	100	84.09	160	134.09	220	184.09	280	234.09	340	284.09	390	325.75	440	367.42	490	409.09
41	34.92	101	84.92	161	134.92	221	184.92	281	234.92	341	284.92	391	326.59	441	368.25	491	409.92
42	35.75	102	85.75	162	135.75	222	185.75	282	235.75	342	285.75	392	327.42	442	369.09	492	410.75
43	36.59	103	86.59	163	136.59	223	186.59	283	236.59	343	286.59	393	328.25	443	369.92	493	411.59
44	37.42	104	87.42	164	137.42	224	187.42	284	237.42	344	287.42	394	329.09	444	370.75	494	412.42
45	38.25	105	88.25	165	138.25	225	188.25	285	238.25	345	288.25	395	329.92	445	371.59	495	413.25
46	39.09	106	89.09	166	139.09	226	189.09	286	239.09	346	289.09	396	330.75	446	372.42	496	414.09
47	39.92	107	89.92	167	139.92	227	189.92	287	239.92	347	289.92	397	331.59	447	373.25	497	414.92
48	40.75	108	90.75	168	140.75	228	190.75	288	240.75	348	290.75	398	332.42	448	374.09	498	415.75
49	41.59	109	91.59	169	141.59	229	191.59	289	241.59	349	291.59	399	333.25	449	374.92	499	416.59
50	42.42	110	92.42	170	142.42	230	192.42	290	242.42	350	292.42	400	334.09	450	375.75	500	417.42
51	43.25	111	93.25	171	143.25	231	193.25	291	243.25								
52	44.09	112	94.09	172	144.09	232	194.09	292	244.09								
53	44.92	113	94.92	173	144.92	233	194.92	293	244.92								
54	45.75	114	95.75	174	145.75	234	195.75	294	245.75								
55	46.59	115	96.59	175	146.59	235	196.59	295	246.59								
56	47.42	116	97.42	176	147.42	236	197.42	296	247.42								
57	48.25	117	98.25	177	148.25	237	198.25	297	248.25								
58	49.09	118	99.09	178	149.09	238	199.09	298	249.09								
59	49.92	119	99.92	179	149.92	239	199.92	299	249.92								
60	50.75	120	100.75	180	150.75	240	200.75	300	250.75								

Pay adjustment where code exceeds 500

1. Where the code is in the range 501 to **1000** inclusive proceed as follows:

   a. Subtract **500** from the code and use the balance of the code to obtain a pay adjustment figure from the table above.

   b. Add this pay adjustment figure to the figure given in the box alongside to obtain the figure of total adjustment to date   * | 416.67 |

2. Where the **code exceeds 1000** follow the instructions on **page 2**.

TABLE A - PAY ADJUSTMENT Month 2

May 6 to June 5

Code	Total pay adjustment to date £	Code	Total pay adjustment to date £	Code	Total pay adjustment to date £	Code	Total pay adjustment to date £	Code	Total pay adjustment to date £	Code	Total pay adjustment to date £	Code	Total pay adjustment to date £	Code	Total pay adjustment to date £	Code	Total pay adjustment to date £
0	NIL																
1	3.18	61	103.18	121	203.18	181	303.18	241	403.18	301	503.18	351	586.50	401	669.84	451	753.18
2	4.84	62	104.84	122	204.84	182	304.84	242	404.84	302	504.84	352	588.18	402	671.50	452	754.84
3	6.50	63	106.50	123	206.50	183	306.50	243	406.50	303	506.50	353	589.84	403	673.18	453	756.50
4	8.18	64	108.18	124	208.18	184	308.18	244	408.18	304	508.18	354	591.50	404	674.84	454	758.18
5	9.84	65	109.84	125	209.84	185	309.84	245	409.84	305	509.84	355	593.18	405	676.50	455	759.84
6	11.50	66	111.50	126	211.50	186	311.50	246	411.50	306	511.50	356	594.84	406	678.18	456	761.50
7	13.18	67	113.18	127	213.18	187	313.18	247	413.18	307	513.18	357	596.50	407	679.84	457	763.18
8	14.84	68	114.84	128	214.84	188	314.84	248	414.84	308	514.84	358	598.18	408	681.50	458	764.84
9	16.50	69	116.50	129	216.50	189	316.50	249	416.50	309	516.50	359	599.84	409	683.18	459	766.50
10	18.18	70	118.18	130	218.18	190	318.18	250	418.18	310	518.18	360	601.50	410	684.84	460	768.18
11	19.84	71	119.84	131	219.84	191	319.84	251	419.84	311	519.84	361	603.18	411	686.50	461	769.84
12	21.50	72	121.50	132	221.50	192	321.50	252	421.50	312	521.50	362	604.84	412	688.18	462	771.50
13	23.18	73	123.18	133	223.18	193	323.18	253	423.18	313	523.18	363	606.50	413	689.84	463	773.18
14	24.84	74	124.84	134	224.84	194	324.84	254	424.84	314	524.84	364	608.18	414	691.50	464	774.84
15	26.50	75	126.50	135	226.50	195	326.50	255	426.50	315	526.50	365	609.84	415	693.18	465	776.50
16	28.18	76	128.18	136	228.18	196	328.18	256	428.18	316	528.18	366	611.50	416	694.84	466	778.18
17	29.84	77	129.84	137	229.84	197	329.84	257	429.84	317	529.84	367	613.18	417	696.50	467	779.84
18	31.50	78	131.50	138	231.50	198	331.50	258	431.50	318	531.50	368	614.84	418	698.18	468	781.50
19	33.18	79	133.18	139	233.18	199	333.18	259	433.18	319	533.18	369	616.50	419	699.84	469	783.18
20	34.84	80	134.84	140	234.84	200	334.84	260	434.84	320	534.84	370	618.18	420	701.50	470	784.84
21	36.50	81	136.50	141	236.50	201	336.50	261	436.50	321	536.50	371	619.84	421	703.18	471	786.50
22	38.18	82	138.18	142	238.18	202	338.18	262	438.18	322	538.18	372	621.50	422	704.84	472	788.18
23	39.84	83	139.84	143	239.84	203	339.84	263	439.84	323	539.84	373	623.18	423	706.50	473	789.84
24	41.50	84	141.50	144	241.50	204	341.50	264	441.50	324	541.50	374	624.84	424	708.18	474	791.50
25	43.18	85	143.18	145	243.18	205	343.18	265	443.18	325	543.18	375	626.50	425	709.84	475	793.18
26	44.84	86	144.84	146	244.84	206	344.84	266	444.84	326	544.84	376	628.18	426	711.50	476	794.84
27	46.50	87	146.50	147	246.50	207	346.50	267	446.50	327	546.50	377	629.84	427	713.18	477	796.50
28	48.18	88	148.18	148	248.18	208	348.18	268	448.18	328	548.18	378	631.50	428	714.84	478	798.18
29	49.84	89	149.84	149	249.84	209	349.84	269	449.84	329	549.84	379	633.18	429	716.50	479	799.84
30	51.50	90	151.50	150	251.50	210	351.50	270	451.50	330	551.50	380	634.84	430	718.18	480	801.50
31	53.18	91	153.18	151	253.18	211	353.18	271	453.18	331	553.18	381	636.50	431	719.84	481	803.18
32	54.84	92	154.84	152	254.84	212	354.84	272	454.84	332	554.84	382	638.18	432	721.50	482	804.84
33	56.50	93	156.50	153	256.50	213	356.50	273	456.50	333	556.50	383	639.84	433	723.18	483	806.50
34	58.18	94	158.18	154	258.18	214	358.18	274	458.18	334	558.18	384	641.50	434	724.84	484	808.18
35	59.84	95	159.84	155	259.84	215	359.84	275	459.84	335	559.84	385	643.18	435	726.50	485	809.84
36	61.50	96	161.50	156	261.50	216	361.50	276	461.50	336	561.50	386	644.84	436	728.18	486	811.50
37	63.18	97	163.18	157	263.18	217	363.18	277	463.18	337	563.18	387	646.50	437	729.84	487	813.18
38	64.84	98	164.84	158	264.84	218	364.84	278	464.84	338	564.84	388	648.18	438	731.50	488	814.84
39	66.50	99	166.50	159	266.50	219	366.50	279	466.50	339	566.50	389	649.84	439	733.18	489	816.50
40	68.18	100	168.18	160	268.18	220	368.18	280	468.18	340	568.18	390	651.50	440	734.84	490	818.18
41	69.84	101	169.84	161	269.84	221	369.84	281	469.84	341	569.84	391	653.18	441	736.50	491	819.84
42	71.50	102	171.50	162	271.50	222	371.50	282	471.50	342	571.50	392	654.84	442	738.18	492	821.50
43	73.18	103	173.18	163	273.18	223	373.18	283	473.18	343	573.18	393	656.50	443	739.84	493	823.18
44	74.84	104	174.84	164	274.84	224	374.84	284	474.84	344	574.84	394	658.18	444	741.50	494	824.84
45	76.50	105	176.50	165	276.50	225	376.50	285	476.50	345	576.50	395	659.84	445	743.18	495	826.50
46	78.18	106	178.18	166	278.18	226	378.18	286	478.18	346	578.18	396	661.50	446	744.84	496	828.18
47	79.84	107	179.84	167	279.84	227	379.84	287	479.84	347	579.84	397	663.18	447	746.50	497	829.84
48	81.50	108	181.50	168	281.50	228	381.50	288	481.50	348	581.50	398	664.84	448	748.18	498	831.50
49	83.18	109	183.18	169	283.18	229	383.18	289	483.18	349	583.18	399	666.50	449	749.84	499	833.18
50	84.84	110	184.84	170	284.84	230	384.84	290	484.84	350	584.84	400	668.18	450	751.50	500	834.84
51	86.50	111	186.50	171	286.50	231	386.50	291	486.50								
52	88.18	112	188.18	172	288.18	232	388.18	292	488.18								
53	89.84	113	189.84	173	289.84	233	389.84	293	489.84								
54	91.50	114	191.50	174	291.50	234	391.50	294	491.50								
55	93.18	115	193.18	175	293.18	235	393.18	295	493.18								
56	94.84	116	194.84	176	294.84	236	394.84	296	494.84								
57	96.50	117	196.50	177	296.50	237	396.50	297	496.50								
58	98.18	118	198.18	178	298.18	238	398.18	298	498.18								
59	99.84	119	199.84	179	299.84	239	399.84	299	499.84								
60	101.50	120	201.50	180	301.50	240	401.50	300	501.50								

Pay adjustment where code exceeds 500

1. Where the code is in the range 501 to **1000** inclusive proceed as follows:

   a. Subtract **500** from the code and use the balance of the code to obtain a pay adjustment figure from the table above.

   b. Add this pay adjustment figure to the figure given in the box alongside to obtain the figure of total adjustment to date   *   833.34

2. Where the code **exceeds 1000** follow the instructions on **page 2**.

Which Tax Table to Use?

For Code BR use Tables B *Tax at 23%* on pages 8 and 9
For Code D0 use Table D on Page 11
For other codes:-

Pay at Monthly rates

1			2			3		
Use table LR (Page 5) when the **total taxable pay** to date **does not exceed**			Use Tables B (Pages 8 **and** 9) when the **total taxable pay** to date **exceeds** the Column 1 figure **but does not exceed**			Use Tables C and D (pages 10 and 11) when the **total taxable pay** to date **exceeds**		
Month No.		£	Month No		£	Month No		£
1	does not exceed	359	1	does not exceed	2259	1	exceeds	2259
2		717	2		4517	2		4517
3		1075	3		6775	3		6775
4		1434	4		9034	4		9034
5		1792	5		11292	5		11292
6		2150	6		13550	6		13550
7		2509	7		15809	7		15809
8		2867	8		18067	8		18067
9		3225	9		20325	9		20325
10		3584	10		22584	10		22584
11		3942	11		24842	11		24842
12		4300	12		27100	12		27100

Table LR (Tax at 20%)   *Pages 2 and 3 tell you when to use this table*

Tax Due on Taxable Pay from £100 to £4300			Tax Due on Taxable Pay from £1 to £99					Where the exact amount of taxable pay is not shown, add together the figures for two (or more) entries to make up the amount of taxable pay to the nearest £1 below
Total TAXABLE PAY to date	Total TAX DUE to date		Total TAXABLE PAY to date	Total TAX DUE to date		Total TAXABLE PAY to date	Total TAX DUE to date	
£	£		£	£		£	£	
100	20.00		1	0.20		50	10.00	
200	40.00		2	0.40		51	10.20	
300	60.00		3	0.60		52	10.40	
400	80.00		4	0.80		53	10.60	
500	100.00		5	1.00		54	10.80	
600	120.00		6	1.20		55	11.00	
700	140.00		7	1.40		56	11.20	
800	160.00		8	1.60		57	11.40	
900	180.00		9	1.80		58	11.60	
1000	200.00		10	2.00		59	11.80	
1100	220.00		11	2.20		60	12.00	
1200	240.00		12	2.40		61	12.20	
1300	260.00		13	2.60		62	12.40	
1400	280.00		14	2.80		63	12.60	
1500	300.00		15	3.00		64	12.80	
1600	320.00		16	3.20		65	13.00	
1700	340.00		17	3.40		66	13.20	
1800	360.00		18	3.60		67	13.40	
1900	380.00		19	3.80		68	13.60	
2000	400.00		20	4.00		69	13.80	
2100	420.00		21	4.20		70	14.00	
2200	440.00		22	4.40		71	14.20	
2300	460.00		23	4.60		72	14.40	
2400	480.00		24	4.80		73	14.60	
2500	500.00		25	5.00		74	14.80	
2600	520.00		26	5.20		75	15.00	
2700	540.00		27	5.40		76	15.20	
2800	560.00		28	5.60		77	15.40	
2900	580.00		29	5.80		78	15.60	
3000	600.00		30	6.00		79	15.80	
3100	620.00		31	6.20		80	16.00	
3200	640.00		32	6.40		81	16.20	
3300	660.00		33	6.60		82	16.40	
3400	680.00		34	6.80		83	16.60	
3500	700.00		35	7.00		84	16.80	
3600	720.00		36	7.20		85	17.00	
3700	740.00		37	7.40		86	17.20	
3800	760.00		38	7.60		87	17.40	
3900	780.00		39	7.80		88	17.60	
4000	800.00		40	8 00		89	17.80	
4100	820.00		41	8.20		90	18.00	
4200	840.00		42	8.40		91	18.20	
4300	860.00		43	8.60		92	18.40	
			44	8.80		93	18.60	
			45	9.00		94	18.80	
			46	9.20		95	19.00	
			47	9.40		96	19.20	
			48	9.60		97	19.40	
			49	9.80		98	19.60	
						99	19.80	

Remember to use the green Subtraction Tables on Page 9

Tables B Tax at 23%   *Pages 2 and 3 tell you when to use these tables*

<table>
<tr><td colspan="10">Tax Due on Taxable Pay from £100 to £27,100</td><td rowspan="3">Where the exact amount of taxable pay is not shown, add together the figures for two (or more) entries to make up the amount of taxable pay to the nearest £1 below</td></tr>
<tr>
<td>Total TAXABLE PAY to date</td><td>Total TAX DUE to date</td>
<td>Total TAXABLE PAY to date</td><td>Total TAX DUE to date</td>
<td>Total TAXABLE PAY to date</td><td>Total TAX DUE to date</td>
<td>Total TAXABLE PAY to date</td><td>Total TAX DUE to date</td>
<td>Total TAXABLE PAY to date</td><td>Total TAX DUE to date</td>
</tr>
<tr>
<td>£</td><td>£</td><td>£</td><td>£</td><td>£</td><td>£</td><td>£</td><td>£</td><td>£</td><td>£</td>
</tr>
<tr><td>100</td><td>23.00</td><td>5600</td><td>1288.00</td><td>11100</td><td>2553.00</td><td>16600</td><td>3818.00</td><td>22100</td><td>5083.00</td></tr>
<tr><td>200</td><td>46.00</td><td>5700</td><td>1311.00</td><td>11200</td><td>2576.00</td><td>16700</td><td>3841.00</td><td>22200</td><td>5106.00</td></tr>
<tr><td>300</td><td>69.00</td><td>5800</td><td>1334.00</td><td>11300</td><td>2599.00</td><td>16800</td><td>3864.00</td><td>22300</td><td>5129.00</td></tr>
<tr><td>400</td><td>92.00</td><td>5900</td><td>1357.00</td><td>11400</td><td>2622.00</td><td>16900</td><td>3887.00</td><td>22400</td><td>5152.00</td></tr>
<tr><td>500</td><td>115.00</td><td>6000</td><td>1380.00</td><td>11500</td><td>2645.00</td><td>17000</td><td>3910.00</td><td>22500</td><td>5175.00</td></tr>
<tr><td>600</td><td>138.00</td><td>6100</td><td>1403.00</td><td>11600</td><td>2668.00</td><td>17100</td><td>3933.00</td><td>22600</td><td>5198.00</td></tr>
<tr><td>700</td><td>161.00</td><td>6200</td><td>1426.00</td><td>11700</td><td>2691.00</td><td>17200</td><td>3956.00</td><td>22700</td><td>5221.00</td></tr>
<tr><td>800</td><td>184.00</td><td>6300</td><td>1449.00</td><td>11800</td><td>2714.00</td><td>17300</td><td>3979.00</td><td>22800</td><td>5244.00</td></tr>
<tr><td>900</td><td>207.00</td><td>6400</td><td>1472.00</td><td>11900</td><td>2737.00</td><td>17400</td><td>4002.00</td><td>22900</td><td>5267.00</td></tr>
<tr><td>1000</td><td>230.00</td><td>6500</td><td>1495.00</td><td>12000</td><td>2760.00</td><td>17500</td><td>4025.00</td><td>23000</td><td>5290.00</td></tr>
<tr><td>1100</td><td>253.00</td><td>6600</td><td>1518.00</td><td>12100</td><td>2783.00</td><td>17600</td><td>4048.00</td><td>23100</td><td>5313.00</td></tr>
<tr><td>1200</td><td>276.00</td><td>6700</td><td>1541.00</td><td>12200</td><td>2806.00</td><td>17700</td><td>4071.00</td><td>23200</td><td>5336.00</td></tr>
<tr><td>1300</td><td>299.00</td><td>6800</td><td>1564.00</td><td>12300</td><td>2829.00</td><td>17800</td><td>4094.00</td><td>23300</td><td>5359.00</td></tr>
<tr><td>1400</td><td>322.00</td><td>6900</td><td>1587.00</td><td>12400</td><td>2852.00</td><td>17900</td><td>4117.00</td><td>23400</td><td>5382.00</td></tr>
<tr><td>1500</td><td>345.00</td><td>7000</td><td>1610.00</td><td>12500</td><td>2875.00</td><td>18000</td><td>4140.00</td><td>23500</td><td>5405.00</td></tr>
<tr><td>1600</td><td>368.00</td><td>7100</td><td>1633.00</td><td>12600</td><td>2898.00</td><td>18100</td><td>4163.00</td><td>23600</td><td>5428.00</td></tr>
<tr><td>1700</td><td>391.00</td><td>7200</td><td>1656.00</td><td>12700</td><td>2921.00</td><td>18200</td><td>4186.00</td><td>23700</td><td>5451.00</td></tr>
<tr><td>1800</td><td>414.00</td><td>7300</td><td>1679.00</td><td>12800</td><td>2944.00</td><td>18300</td><td>4209.00</td><td>23800</td><td>5474.00</td></tr>
<tr><td>1900</td><td>437.00</td><td>7400</td><td>1702.00</td><td>12900</td><td>2967.00</td><td>18400</td><td>4232.00</td><td>23900</td><td>5497.00</td></tr>
<tr><td>2000</td><td>460.00</td><td>7500</td><td>1725.00</td><td>13000</td><td>2990.00</td><td>18500</td><td>4255.00</td><td>24000</td><td>5520.00</td></tr>
<tr><td>2100</td><td>483.00</td><td>7600</td><td>1748.00</td><td>13100</td><td>3013.00</td><td>18600</td><td>4278.00</td><td>24100</td><td>5543.00</td></tr>
<tr><td>2200</td><td>506.00</td><td>7700</td><td>1771.00</td><td>13200</td><td>3036.00</td><td>18700</td><td>4301.00</td><td>24200</td><td>5566.00</td></tr>
<tr><td>2300</td><td>529.00</td><td>7800</td><td>1794.00</td><td>13300</td><td>3059.00</td><td>18800</td><td>4324.00</td><td>24300</td><td>5589.00</td></tr>
<tr><td>2400</td><td>552.00</td><td>7900</td><td>1817.00</td><td>13400</td><td>3082.00</td><td>18900</td><td>4347.00</td><td>24400</td><td>5612.00</td></tr>
<tr><td>2500</td><td>575.00</td><td>8000</td><td>1840.00</td><td>13500</td><td>3105.00</td><td>19000</td><td>4370.00</td><td>24500</td><td>5635.00</td></tr>
<tr><td>2600</td><td>598.00</td><td>8100</td><td>1863.00</td><td>13600</td><td>3128.00</td><td>19100</td><td>4393.00</td><td>24600</td><td>5658.00</td></tr>
<tr><td>2700</td><td>621.00</td><td>8200</td><td>1886.00</td><td>13700</td><td>3151.00</td><td>19200</td><td>4416.00</td><td>24700</td><td>5681.00</td></tr>
<tr><td>2800</td><td>644.00</td><td>8300</td><td>1909.00</td><td>13800</td><td>3174.00</td><td>19300</td><td>4439.00</td><td>24800</td><td>5704.00</td></tr>
<tr><td>2900</td><td>667.00</td><td>8400</td><td>1932.00</td><td>13900</td><td>3197.00</td><td>19400</td><td>4462.00</td><td>24900</td><td>5727.00</td></tr>
<tr><td>3000</td><td>690.00</td><td>8500</td><td>1955.00</td><td>14000</td><td>3220.00</td><td>19500</td><td>4485.00</td><td>25000</td><td>5750.00</td></tr>
<tr><td>3100</td><td>713.00</td><td>8600</td><td>1978.00</td><td>14100</td><td>3243.00</td><td>19600</td><td>4508.00</td><td>25100</td><td>5773.00</td></tr>
<tr><td>3200</td><td>736.00</td><td>8700</td><td>2001.00</td><td>14200</td><td>3266.00</td><td>19700</td><td>4531.00</td><td>25200</td><td>5796.00</td></tr>
<tr><td>3300</td><td>759.00</td><td>8800</td><td>2024.00</td><td>14300</td><td>3289.00</td><td>19800</td><td>4554.00</td><td>25300</td><td>5819.00</td></tr>
<tr><td>3400</td><td>782.00</td><td>8900</td><td>2047.00</td><td>14400</td><td>3312.00</td><td>19900</td><td>4577.00</td><td>25400</td><td>5842.00</td></tr>
<tr><td>3500</td><td>805.00</td><td>9000</td><td>2070.00</td><td>14500</td><td>3335.00</td><td>20000</td><td>4600.00</td><td>25500</td><td>5865.00</td></tr>
<tr><td>3600</td><td>828.00</td><td>9100</td><td>2093.00</td><td>14600</td><td>3358.00</td><td>20100</td><td>4623.00</td><td>25600</td><td>5888.00</td></tr>
<tr><td>3700</td><td>851.00</td><td>9200</td><td>2116.00</td><td>14700</td><td>3381.00</td><td>20200</td><td>4646.00</td><td>25700</td><td>5911.00</td></tr>
<tr><td>3800</td><td>874.00</td><td>9300</td><td>2139.00</td><td>14800</td><td>3404.00</td><td>20300</td><td>4669.00</td><td>25800</td><td>5934.00</td></tr>
<tr><td>3900</td><td>897.00</td><td>9400</td><td>2162.00</td><td>14900</td><td>3427.00</td><td>20400</td><td>4692.00</td><td>25900</td><td>5957.00</td></tr>
<tr><td>4000</td><td>920.00</td><td>9500</td><td>2185.00</td><td>15000</td><td>3450.00</td><td>20500</td><td>4715.00</td><td>26000</td><td>5980.00</td></tr>
<tr><td>4100</td><td>943.00</td><td>9600</td><td>2208.00</td><td>15100</td><td>3473.00</td><td>20600</td><td>4738.00</td><td>26100</td><td>6003.00</td></tr>
<tr><td>4200</td><td>966.00</td><td>9700</td><td>2231.00</td><td>15200</td><td>3496.00</td><td>20700</td><td>4761.00</td><td>26200</td><td>6026.00</td></tr>
<tr><td>4300</td><td>989.00</td><td>9800</td><td>2254.00</td><td>15300</td><td>3519.00</td><td>20800</td><td>4784.00</td><td>26300</td><td>6049.00</td></tr>
<tr><td>4400</td><td>1012.00</td><td>9900</td><td>2277.00</td><td>15400</td><td>3542.00</td><td>20900</td><td>4807.00</td><td>26400</td><td>6072.00</td></tr>
<tr><td>4500</td><td>1035.00</td><td>10000</td><td>2300.00</td><td>15500</td><td>3565.00</td><td>21000</td><td>4830.00</td><td>26500</td><td>6095.00</td></tr>
<tr><td>4600</td><td>1158.00</td><td>10100</td><td>2323.00</td><td>15600</td><td>3588.00</td><td>21100</td><td>4853.00</td><td>26600</td><td>6118.00</td></tr>
<tr><td>4700</td><td>1081.00</td><td>10200</td><td>2346.00</td><td>15700</td><td>3611.00</td><td>21200</td><td>4876.00</td><td>26700</td><td>6141.00</td></tr>
<tr><td>4800</td><td>1104.00</td><td>10300</td><td>2369.00</td><td>15800</td><td>3634.00</td><td>21300</td><td>4899.00</td><td>26800</td><td>6164.00</td></tr>
<tr><td>4900</td><td>1127.00</td><td>10400</td><td>2392.00</td><td>15900</td><td>3657.00</td><td>21400</td><td>4922.00</td><td>26900</td><td>6187.00</td></tr>
<tr><td>5000</td><td>1150.00</td><td>10500</td><td>2415.00</td><td>16000</td><td>3680.00</td><td>21500</td><td>4945.00</td><td>27000</td><td>6210.00</td></tr>
<tr><td>5100</td><td>1173.00</td><td>10600</td><td>2438.00</td><td>16100</td><td>3703.00</td><td>21600</td><td>4968.00</td><td>27100</td><td>6233.00</td></tr>
<tr><td>5200</td><td>1196.00</td><td>10700</td><td>2461.00</td><td>16200</td><td>3726.00</td><td>21700</td><td>4991.00</td><td></td><td></td></tr>
<tr><td>5300</td><td>1219.00</td><td>10800</td><td>2484.00</td><td>16300</td><td>3749.00</td><td>21800</td><td>5014.00</td><td></td><td></td></tr>
<tr><td>5400</td><td>1242.00</td><td>10900</td><td>2507.00</td><td>16400</td><td>3772.00</td><td>21900</td><td>5037.00</td><td></td><td></td></tr>
<tr><td>5500</td><td>1265.00</td><td>11000</td><td>2530.00</td><td>16500</td><td>3795.00</td><td>22000</td><td>5060.00</td><td></td><td></td></tr>
</table>

Remember to use the green Subtraction Tables below

Tables B Tax at 23%

Tax Due on Taxable Pay from £1 to £99									
Total TAXABLE PAY to date	Total TAX DUE to date	Total TAXABLE PAY to date	Total TAX DUE to date	Total TAXABLE PAY to date	Total TAX DUE to date	Total TAXABLE PAY to date	Total TAX DUE to date	Total TAXABLE PAY to date	Total TAX DUE to date
£	£	£	£	£	£	£	£	£	£
1	0.23	21	4.83	41	9.43	61	14.03	81	18.63
2	0.46	22	5.06	42	9.66	62	14.26	82	18.86
3	0.69	23	5.29	43	9.89	63	14.49	83	19.09
4	0.92	24	5.52	44	10.12	64	14.72	84	19.32
5	1.15	25	5.75	45	10.35	65	14.95	85	19.55
6	1.38	26	5.98	46	10.58	66	15.18	86	19.78
7	1.61	27	6.21	47	10.81	67	15.41	87	20.01
8	1.84	28	6.44	48	11.04	68	15.64	88	20.24
9	2.07	29	6.67	49	11.27	69	15.87	89	20.47
10	2.30	30	6.90	50	11.50	70	16.10	90	20.70
11	2.53	31	7.13	51	11.73	71	16.33	91	20.93
12	2.76	32	7.36	52	11.96	72	16.56	92	21.16
13	2.99	33	7.59	53	12.19	73	16.79	93	21.39
14	3.22	34	7.82	54	12.42	74	17.02	94	21.62
15	3.45	35	8.05	55	12.65	75	17.25	95	21.85
16	3.68	36	8.28	56	12.88	76	17.48	96	22.08
17	3.91	37	8.51	57	13.11	77	17.71	97	22.31
18	4.14	38	8.74	58	13.34	78	17.94	98	22.54
19	4.37	39	8.97	59	13.57	79	18.17	99	22.77
20	4.60	40	9.20	60	13.80	80	18.40		

Where the exact amount of taxable pay is not shown, add together the figures for two (or more) entries to make up the amount of taxable pay to the nearest £1 below

Subtraction Tables - to give Lower Rate Relief

Use the subtraction tables for all ordinary suffix codes and prefix K codes. Do not use the subtraction tables for codes BR and D0.

After you have used Tables B to work out the tax at 23% use the tables below to give the benefit of the 20% rate band. Find the month or week in which the pay day falls and **subtract** the amount shown to arrive at the tax due.

Employee paid at Monthly rates

Month No	Amount to subtract £
1	10.76
2	21.51
3	32.25
4	43.01
5	53.76
6	64.50
7	75.26
8	86.01
9	96.75
10	107.51
11	118.26
12	129.00

Employee paid at Weekly rates

Week No	Amount to subtract £	Week No	Amount to subtract £
1	2.49	27	66.99
2	4.97	28	69.47
3	7.45	29	71.95
4	9.93	30	74.43
5	12.41	31	76.91
6	14.89	32	79.39
7	17.37	33	81.87
8	19.85	34	84.35
		35	86.83
9	22.33		
10	24.81	36	89.31
11	27.29	37	91.79
12	29.77	38	94.27
13	32.25	39	96.76
14	34.74	40	99.24
15	37.22	41	101.72
16	39.70	42	104.20
17	42.18	43	106.68
18	44.66	44	109.16
19	47.14	45	111.64
20	49.62	46	114.12
21	52.10	47	116.60
22	54.58	48	119.08
23	57.06	49	121.56
24	59.54	50	124.04
25	62.02	51	126.52
26	64.50	52	129.00

Table C   *Pages 2 and 3 tell you when to use this table*

Employee paid at Weekly rates

Week No.	If total taxable pay to date exceeds	Total tax due to date
	Col 1 £	Col 2 £
1	522	117.72
2	1043	235.04
3	1564	352.36
4	2085	469.69
5	2606	587.01
6	3127	704.33
7	3649	822.06
8	4170	939.38
9	4691	1056.70
10	5212	1174.03
11	5733	1291.35
12	6254	1408.67
13	6775	1526.00
14	7297	1643.72
15	7818	1761.04
16	8339	1878.36
17	8860	1995.69
18	9381	2113.01
19	9902	2230.33
20	10424	2348.06
21	10945	2465.38
22	11466	2582.70
23	11987	2700.03
24	12508	2817.35
25	13029	2934.67
26	13550	3052.00
27	14072	3169.72
28	14593	3287.04
29	15114	3404.36
30	15635	3521.69
31	16156	3639.01
32	16677	3756.33
33	17199	3874.06
34	17720	3991.38
35	18241	4108.70
36	18762	4226.03
37	19283	4343.35
38	19804	4460.67
39	20325	4578.00
40	20847	4695.72
41	21368	4813.04
42	21889	4930.36
43	22410	5047.69
44	22931	5165.01
45	23452	5282.33
46	23974	5400.06
47	24495	5517.38
48	25016	5634.70
49	25537	5752.03
50	26058	5869.35
51	26579	5986.67
52	27100	6104.00

Plus tax at 40% as shown in Table D on the amount by which the total Taxable Pay to date exceeds the figure in Col. 1

How to use Table C

Example

Employee's code is **419L**
The payment is made in **Week 10**

Pay in the week	£ 700
Previous pay to date	£6300
Total pay to date	£7000
Less free pay in Week 10 (Table A)	£ 807.50
Total taxable pay to date	**£6192.50**

Subtract amount in Col 1 (for Week 10)

£5212 tax due per Col 2   **£1174.03**

Excess (£6192 - £5212) £ 980
therefore tax due per Table D =   **£392.00**

Employee paid at Monthly rates

Month No.	If total taxable pay to date exceeds	Total tax due to date
	Col 1 £	Col 2 £
1	2259	508.93
2	4517	1017.46
3	6775	1526.00
4	9034	2034.93
5	11292	2543.46
6	13550	3052.00
7	15809	3560.93
8	18067	4069.46
9	20325	4578.00
10	22584	5086.93
11	24842	5595.46
12	27100	6104.00

Plus tax at 40% as shown in Table D on the amount by which the total Taxable Pay to date exceeds the figure in Col. 1

Table D

Pages 2 and 3 tell you when to use these tables

(Tax at 40%)

Also to be used for Code D0

Income £	Tax £	Income £	Tax £	Income £	Tax £	Income £	Tax £
1	0.40	50	20.00	100	40.00	6100	2440.00
2	0.80	51	20.40	200	80.00	6200	2480.00
3	1.20	52	20.80	300	120.00	6300	2520.00
4	1.60	53	21.20	400	160.00	6400	2560.00
5	2.00	54	21.60	500	200.00	6500	2600.00
6	2.40	55	22.00	600	240.00	6600	2640.00
7	2.80	56	22.40	700	280.00	6700	2680.00
8	3.20	57	22.80	800	320.00	6800	2720.00
9	3.60	58	23.20	900	360.00	6900	2760.00
10	4.00	59	23.60	1000	400.00	7000	2800.00
11	4.40	60	24.00	1100	440.00	7100	2840.00
12	4.80	61	24.40	1200	480.00	7200	2880.00
13	5.20	62	24.80	1300	520.00	7300	2920.00
14	5.60	63	25.20	1400	560.00	7400	2960.00
15	6.00	64	25.60	1500	600.00	7500	3000.00
16	6.40	65	26.00	1600	640.00	7600	3040.00
17	6.80	66	26.40	1700	680.00	7700	3080.00
18	7.20	67	26.80	1800	720.00	7800	3120.00
19	7.60	68	27.20	1900	760.00	7900	3160.00
20	8.00	69	27.60	2000	800.00	8000	3200.00
21	8.40	70	28.00	2100	840.00	8100	3240.00
22	8.80	71	28.40	2200	880.00	8200	3280.00
23	9.20	72	28.80	2300	920.00	8300	3320.00
24	9.60	73	29.20	2400	960.00	8400	3360.00
25	10.00	74	29.60	2500	1000.00	8500	3400.00
26	10.40	75	30.00	2600	1040.00	8600	3440.00
27	10.80	76	30.40	2700	1080.00	8700	3480.00
28	11.20	77	30.80	2800	1120.00	8800	3520.00
29	11.60	78	31.20	2900	1160.00	8900	3560.00
30	12.00	79	31.60	3000	1200.00	9000	3600.00
31	12.40	80	32.00	3100	1240.00	9100	3640.00
32	12.80	81	32.40	3200	1280.00	9200	3680.00
33	13.20	82	32.80	3300	1320.00	9300	3720.00
34	13.60	83	33.20	3400	1360.00	9400	3760.00
35	14.00	84	33.60	3500	1400.00	9500	3800.00
36	14.40	85	34.00	3600	1440.00	9600	3840.00
37	14.80	86	34.40	3700	1480.00	9700	3880.00
38	15.20	87	34.80	3800	1520.00	9800	3920.00
39	15.60	88	35.20	3900	1560.00	9900	3960.00
40	16.00	89	35.60	4000	1600.00	10000	4000.00
41	16.40	90	36.00	4100	1640.00	20000	8000.00
42	16.80	91	36.40	4200	1680.00	30000	12000.00
43	17.20	92	36.80	4300	1720.00	40000	16000.00
44	17.60	93	37.20	4400	1760.00	50000	20000.00
45	18.00	94	37.60	4500	1800.00	60000	24000.00
46	18.40	95	38.00	4600	1840.00	70000	28000.00
47	18.80	96	38.40	4700	1880.00	80000	32000.00
48	19.20	97	38.80	4800	1920.00	90000	36000.00
49	19.60	98	39.20	4900	1960.00	100000	40000.00
		99	39.60	5000	2000.00	200000	80000.00
				5100	2040.00	300000	120000.00
				5200	2080.00	400000	160000.00
				5300	2120.00	500000	200000.00
				5400	2160.00	600000	240000.00
				5500	2200.00	700000	280000.00
				5600	2240.00	800000	32000.00
				5700	2280.00	900000	36000.00
				5800	2320.00	1000000	40000.00
				5900	2360.00		
				6000	2400.00		

Where the exact amount of taxable pay is not shown, add together the figures for two (or more) entries to make up the amount of taxable pay to the nearest £1 below

Contribution table letter

A

Monthly table

Earnings on which employee's contributions payable 1a	Total of employee's and employer's contributions payable 1b	Employee's contributions payable 1c	▼ Employer's contributions	Earnings on which employee's contributions payable 1a	Total of employee's and employer's contributions payable 1b	Employee's contributions payable 1c	▼ Employer's contributions
£	£	£	£	£	£	£	£
1070	192.16	84.96	107.20	1230	224.16	100.96	123.20
1074	192.96	85.36	107.60	1234	224.96	101.36	123.60
1078	193.76	85.76	108.00	1238	225.76	101.76	124.00
1082	194.56	86.16	108.40	1242	226.56	102.16	124.40
1086	195.36	86.56	108.80	1246	227.36	102.56	124.80
1090	196.16	86.96	109.20	1250	228.16	102.96	125.20
1094	196.96	87.36	109.60	1254	228.96	103.36	125.60
1098	197.76	87.76	110.00	1258	229.76	103.76	126.00
1102	198.56	88.16	110.40	1262	230.56	104.16	126.40
1106	199.36	88.56	110.80	1266	231.36	104.56	126.80
1110	200.16	88.96	111.20	1270	232.16	104.96	127.20
1114	200.96	89.36	111.60	1274	232.96	105.36	127.60
1118	201.76	89.76	112.00	1278	233.76	105.76	128.00
1122	202.56	90.16	112.40	1282	234.56	106.16	128.40
1126	203.36	90.56	112.80	1286	235.36	106.56	128.80
1130	204.16	90.96	113.20	1290	236.16	106.96	129.20
1134	204.96	91.36	113.60	1294	236.96	107.36	129.60
1138	205.76	91.76	114.00	1298	237.76	107.76	130.00
1142	206.56	92.16	114.40	1302	238.56	108.16	130.40
1146	207.36	92.56	114.80	1306	239.36	108.56	130.80
1150	208.16	92.96	115.20	1310	240.16	108.96	131.20
1154	208.96	93.36	115.60	1314	240.96	109.36	131.60
1158	209.76	93.76	116.00	1318	241.76	109.76	132.00
1162	210.56	94.16	116.40	1322	242.56	110.16	132.40
1166	211.36	94.56	116.80	1326	243.36	110.56	132.80
1170	212.16	94.96	117.20	1330	244.16	110.96	133.20
1174	212.96	95.36	117.60	1334	244.96	111.36	133.60
1178	213.76	95.76	118.00	1338	245.76	111.76	134.00
1182	214.56	96.16	118.40	1342	246.56	112.16	134.40
1186	215.36	96.56	118.80	1346	247.36	112.56	134.80
1190	216.16	96.96	119.20	1350	248.16	112.96	135.20
1194	216.96	97.36	119.60	1354	248.96	113.36	135.60
1198	217.76	97.76	120.00	1358	249.76	113.76	136.00
1202	218.56	98.16	120.40	1362	250.56	114.16	136.40
1206	219.36	98.56	120.80	1366	251.36	114.56	136.80
1210	220.16	98.96	121.20	1370	252.16	114.96	137.20
1214	220.96	99.36	121.60	1374	252.96	115.36	137.60
1218	221.76	99.76	122.00	1378	253.76	115.76	138.00
1222	222.56	100.16	122.40	1382	254.56	116.16	138.40
1226	223.36	100.56	122.80	1386	255.36	116.56	138.80

▼ for information only - do not enter on Deductions Working Sheet, form P11

Monthly table

Contribution table letter

Earnings on which employee's contributions payable 1a	Total of employee's and employer's contributions payable 1b	Employee's contributions payable 1c	▼ Employer's contributions	Earnings on which employee's contributions payable 1a	Total of employee's and employer's contributions payable 1b	Employee's contributions payable 1c	▼ Employer's contributions
£	£	£	£	£	£	£	£
1390	256.16	116.96	139.20	1550	288.16	132.96	155.20
1394	256.96	117.36	139.60	1554	288.96	133.36	155.60
1398	257.76	117.76	140.00	1558	289.76	133.76	156.00
1402	258.56	118.16	140.40	1562	290.56	134.16	156.40
1406	259.36	118.56	140.80	1566	291.36	134.56	156.80
1410	260.16	118.96	141.20	1570	292.16	134.96	157.20
1414	260.96	119.36	141.60	1574	292.96	135.36	157.60
1418	261.76	119.76	142.00	1578	293.76	135.76	158.00
1422	262.56	120.16	142.40	1582	294.56	136.16	158.40
1426	263.36	120.56	142.80	1586	295.36	136.56	158.80
1430	264.16	120.96	143.20	1590	296.16	136.96	159.20
1434	264.96	121.36	143.60	1594	296.96	137.36	159.60
1438	265.76	121.76	144.00	1598	297.76	137.76	160.00
1442	266.56	122.16	144.40	1602	298.56	138.16	160.40
1446	267.36	122.56	144.80	1606	299.36	138.56	160.80
1450	268.16	122.96	145.20	1610	300.16	138.96	161.20
1454	268.96	123.36	145.60	1614	300.96	139.36	161.60
1458	269.76	123.76	146.00	1618	301.76	139.76	162.00
1462	270.56	124.16	146.40	1622	302.56	140.16	162.40
1466	271.36	124.56	146.80	1626	303.36	140.56	162.80
1470	272.16	124.96	147.20	1630	304.16	140.96	163.20
1474	272.96	125.36	147.60	1634	304.96	141.36	163.60
1478	273.76	125.76	148.00	1638	305.76	141.76	164.00
1482	274.56	126.16	148.40	1642	306.56	142.16	164.40
1486	275.36	126.56	148.80	1646	307.36	142.56	164.80
1490	276.16	126.96	149.20	1650	308.16	142.96	165.20
1494	276.96	127.36	149.60	1654	308.96	143.36	165.60
1498	277.76	127.76	150.00	1658	309.76	143.76	166.00
1502	278.56	128.16	150.40	1662	310.56	144.16	166.40
1506	279.36	128.56	150.80	1666	311.36	144.56	166.80
1510	280.16	128.96	151.20	1670	312.16	144.96	167.20
1514	280.96	129.36	151.60	1674	312.96	145.36	167.60
1518	281.76	129.76	152.00	1678	313.76	145.76	168.00
1522	282.56	130.16	152.40	1682	314.56	146.16	168.40
1526	283.36	130.56	152.80	1686	315.36	146.56	168.80
1530	284.16	130.96	153.20	1690	316.16	146.96	169.20
1534	284.96	131.36	153.60	1694	316.96	147.36	169.60
1538	285.76	131.76	154.00	1698	317.76	147.76	170.00
1542	286.56	132.16	154.40	1702	318.56	148.16	170.40
1546	287.36	132.56	154.80	1706	319.36	148.56	170.80

▼ for information only - do not enter on Deductions Working Sheet, form P11

Contribution table letter

B

Weekly table for not contracted-out reduced rate contributions for use from 6 April 1998 to 5 April 1999

Use this table for -

► married women or widows who have the right to pay reduced rate employee's contributions for whom you hold a valid certificate CA4139, CF383 or CF380A

Do not use this table for -

► women aged 60 or over, see Table C

► women for whom you hold form CA2700, see Table C

Completing Deductions Working Sheet, form P11 or substitute -

► enter 'B' in the space provided in the 'End of Year Summary' box of form P11

► copy the figures in columns 1b and 1c of the table to columns 1b and 1c of form P11 on the line next to the tax week in which the employee is paid. You may copy the figure in column 1a of the table to column 1a of form P11 if you wish

If the exact gross pay is not shown in the table, use the next smaller figure shown.

Earnings on which employee's contributions payable 1a	Total of employee's and employer's contributions payable 1b	Employee's contributions payable 1c	▼ Employer's contributions	Earnings on which employee's contributions payable 1a	Total of employee's and employer's contributions payable 1b	Employee's contributions payable 1c	▼ Employer's contributions
£	£	£	£	£	£	£	£
64	4.38	2.46	1.92	84	5.78	3.25	2.53
65	4.48	2.52	1.96	85	5.85	3.29	2.56
66	4.55	2.56	1.99	86	5.92	3.33	2.59
67	4.62	2.60	2.02	87	5.99	3.37	2.62
68	4.69	2.64	2.05	88	6.06	3.41	2.65
69	4.76	2.68	2.08	89	6.13	3.45	2.68
70	4.82	2.71	2.11	90	6.19	3.48	2.71
71	4.89	2.75	2.14	91	6.26	3.52	2.74
72	4.96	2.79	2.17	92	6.33	3.56	2.77
73	5.03	2.83	2.20	93	6.40	3.60	2.80
74	5.10	2.87	2.23	94	6.47	3.64	2.83
75	5.17	2.91	2.26	95	6.54	3.68	2.86
76	5.24	2.95	2.29	96	6.61	3.72	2.89
77	5.30	2.98	2.32	97	6.67	3.75	2.92
78	5.37	3.02	2.35	98	6.74	3.79	2.95
79	5.44	3.06	2.38	99	6.81	3.83	2.98
80	5.51	3.10	2.41	100	6.88	3.87	3.01
81	5.58	3.14	2.44	101	6.95	3.91	3.04
82	5.65	3.18	2.47	102	7.02	3.95	3.07
83	5.71	3.21	2.50	103	7.08	3.98	3.10

▼ for information only - do not enter on Deductions Working Sheet, form P11

Weekly table for
not contracted-out employer
only contributions for use
from
6 April 1998 to 5 April 1999

Use this table for -

► employees who are State pension age or over, for whom you hold a valid certificate CA4140 or CF384

► women for whom you hold a valid certificate CA2700

Completing Deductions Working Sheet, form P11 or substitute -

► enter 'C' in the space provided in the 'End of Year Summary' box of form P11

► copy the figures in column 1b of the table to column 1b of form P11 on the line next to the tax week in which the employee is paid. You may copy the figure in column 1a of the table to column 1a of form P11 if you wish

If the exact gross pay is not shown in the table, use the next smaller figure shown.

Earnings on which contributions payable 1a	Total of employer's contributions payable 1b	Earnings on which contributions payable 1a	Total of employer's contributions payable 1b	Earnings on which contributions payable 1a	Total of employer's contributions payable 1b	Earnings on which contributions payable 1a	Total of employer's contributions payable 1b
£	£	£	£	£	£	£	£
64	1.92	89	2.68	114	5.72	139	6.97
65	1.96	90	2.71	115	5.77	140	7.02
66	1.99	91	2.74	116	5.82	141	7.07
67	2.02	92	2.77	117	5.87	142	7.12
68	2.05	93	2.80	118	5.92	143	7.17
69	2.08	94	2.83	119	5.97	144	7.22
70	2.11	95	2.86	120	6.02	145	7.27
71	2.14	96	2.89	121	6.07	146	7.32
72	2.17	97	2.92	122	6.12	147	7.37
73	2.20	98	2.95	123	6.17	148	7.42
74	2.23	99	2.98	124	6.22	149	7.47
75	2.26	100	3.01	125	6.27	150	7.52
76	2.29	101	3.04	126	6.32	151	7.57
77	2.32	102	3.07	127	6.37	152	7.62
78	2.35	103	3.10	128	6.42	153	7.67
79	2.38	104	3.13	129	6.47	154	7.72
80	2.41	105	3.16	130	6.52	155	10.88
81	2.44	106	3.19	131	6.57	156	10.95
82	2.47	107	2.22	132	6.62	157	11.02
83	2.50	108	2.25	133	6.67	158	11.09
84	2.53	109	3.28	134	6.72	159	11.16
85	2.56	110	5.52	135	6.77	160	11.23
86	2.59	111	5.57	136	6.82	161	11.30
87	2.62	112	5.62	137	6.87	162	11.37
88	2.65	113	5.67	138	6.92	163	11.44

Statutory Sick Pay daily rates table

Unrounded daily rates* £	No of QDs in week	1 £	2 £	3 £	4 £	5 £	6 £	7 £
8.2428	7	8.25	16.49	24.73	32.98	41.22	49.46	57.70
9.6166	6	9.62	19.24	28.85	38.47	48.09	57.70	
11.5400	5	11.54	23.08	34.62	46.16	57.70		
14.4250	4	14.43	28.85	43.28	57.70			
19.2333	3	19.24	38.47	57.70				
28.8500	2	28.85	57.70					
57.7000	1	57.70						

* Unrounded rates are included for employers with computerised payroll systems

Answers to Questions

Exercise 1   (Page 10)

1 Travel from home to work – not tax allowable.

2 Equipment depreciation – not tax allowable (capital allowances instead).

3 Interest on loan from relative – allowable provided the loan is used in the business and interest is at a commercial rate.

4 Cost of guard dog – allowable provided dog genuinely acts as a guard dog, not allowable if it is simply a pet.

5 Use of home telephone – that part relating to work is allowable. Records should be kept.

6 Owner's drawings – not allowable.

7 Speeding fine – not allowable (illegal act).

8 Owner's car insurance – partly allowable in proportion to business/ private use.

9 Accountant's charges – allowable when preparing or auditing accounts. Special investigation and personal work not allowed.

10 Entertaining foreign businessmen – no entertaining allowed at all.

11 Owner's pension fund – yes, provided the contributions are within the age band.

Exercise 2 (Page 18)

	£	Tax
Profit	26000	
Less personal allowance	(4195)	
	21805	
First £4,300 taxed @ 20%	4300	860.00
Next £17,505 @ 23%	17505	4026.15
Total tax payable		4886.15
Less tax credit for child allowance £1,900 @ 15%		(285.00)
Tax payable		4601.15

Did you remember to allow the child allowance as a tax credit at 15%?

Exercise 3 (Page 21)

Tax Year	Accounting Period	Profit Assessed £
1996/97	1.6.96 – 5.4.97	20,000 (ie 10/12 x £24,000)
1997/98	1.6.96 – 31.5.97	24,000 (ie first 12 months profits)
1998/99	1.6.97 – 31.5.98	26,000 (ie year ended 31.5.98 ends in 1998/99 tax year)

Exercise 4 (Pages 36–38)

Bill and Ben's Tax Calculation

	£	£
Net profit per accounts		43110
Add disallowed items:		
Owners' Drawings	22000	
Golf Club	200	
Depreciation	2200	
Christmas Gifts	160	
School Fees	4000	
Partners' Pension Fund	2200	
		30760
		73870
Less:		
Capital Allowances	1900	
		1900
Taxable Profit		71970
Profit Share	Bill (60%)	43182
	Ben (40%)	28788

Continued overleaf

Exercise 4 (Contd)

	Bill £	Tax £	Ben £	Tax £
Partner's share of profit	43182		28788	
Less				
Personal allowance	(4195)		(4195)	
Pension Contribution	(1100)		(1100)	
	37887		23493	
Tax @ 20%	4300	860.00	4300	860.00
	33587		19193	
Tax @ 23%	22800	5244.00	19193	4414.39
	10787			
Tax @ 40%	10787	4314.80		
Total tax		10418.80		5274.39
Less Tax credit for marriage				
allce £1,900 @ 15%		(285.00)		(285.00)
Tax payable		10133.80		4989.39

Exercise 5 (Page 50)

(i)   £26.25
(ii)   £176.75
(iii) £14.89

Exercise 6 (Page 52)

Remember the tax return is properly based on the tax point, not on the invoice date.

Value of Sales (excl vat)	100	6000
	101	5000
	102	12000
		23000

Value of Purchases (excl vat)	1	1300
	2	1500
	3	4000
	4	6600
		13400

Vat on Outputs £23,000 @ 17½% =   4025

Vat on Inputs £13,400 @ 17½%   =   (2345)

Vat payable to HMC&E   1680

Continued overleaf

Value Added Tax Return
For the period

HM Customs
and Excise

For Official Use

Exercise 6 (Page 52)

Registration Number | Period

You could be liable to a financial penalty if your completed return and all the VAT payable are not received by the due date.

Due date:

For Official Use

Your VAT Office telephone number is

Before you fill in this form please read the notes on the back and the VAT leaflet *"Filling in your VAT return"*. Fill in all boxes clearly and write 'none' where necessary. Don't put as dash or leave any box blank. If there are no pence write **"00"** in the pence column.
Do not enter more than one amount in any box.

For official use		£	p
VAT due in this period on **sales** and other outputs	1	4025	00
VAT due in this period on **acquisitions** from other **EC Member States**	2	None	
Total VAT due **(the sum of boxes 1 and 2)**	3	4025	00
VAT reclaimed in this period on **purchases** and other inputs (including acquisitions from the EC)	4	2345	00
Net VAT to be paid to Customs or reclaimed by you **(Difference between boxes 3 and 4)**	5	1680	00
Total value of **sales** and all other outputs excluding any VAT. **Include your box 8 figure**	6	23000	00
Total value of **purchases** and all other outputs excluding any VAT. **Include your box 9 figure** inputs excluding	7	13400	00
Total value of all **supplies** of goods and related services, excluding any VAT, to other **EC Member States**	8		00
Total value of all **acquisitions** of goods and related services, excluding any VAT, from other **EC Member States**	9		00

Retail schemes. If you have used any of the schemes in the period covered by this return, enter the relevant letter(s) in this box.

If you are enclosing a payment please tick this box.

DECLARATION: You, or someone on your behalf, must sign below.
I,...declare that the
(Full name of signatory in BLOCK LETTERS)
information given above is true and complete.
Signature...Date.............19......

B

A false declaration can result in prosecution.

CD 2859/N3(08/93)   F3790 (Febuary1994)
VAT 100

Exercise 7 (Page 74)

Month no	Week no	Pay in the week or month including Statutory Sick Pay/Statutory Maternity Pay 2 £	Total pay to date 3 £	Total free pay to date (Table A) 4a £	K codes only — Total 'additional pay' to date (Table A) 4b £	Total taxable pay to date i.e. column 3 minus column 4a or column 3 plus column 4b 5 £	Total tax due to date as shown by Taxable Pay Tables 6 £	K codes only — Tax due at end of current period Mark refunds 'R' 6a £	K codes only — Regulatory limit i.e. 50% of column 2 entry 6b £	Tax deducted or refunded in the week or month Mark refunds 'R' 7 £	K codes only — Tax not deducted owing to the Regulatory limit 8 £	For employer's use
	1											
	2											
	3											
1	4	1100 00	1100 00	437 42		662 58	141 50			141 50		
	5											
	6											
	7											
2	8	1200 00	2300 00	874 84		1425 16	306 24			164 74		
	9											
	10											
	11											
	12											
3	13	1400 00	3700 00	1312 26		2387 74	516 76			210 52		
	14											
	15											
	16											
4	17	1250 00	4950 00	1749 68		3200 32	692 99			176 23		
	18											
	19											
	20											
5	21	1500 00	6450 00	2187 10		4262 90	926 50			233 51		
	22											
	23											
	24											
	25											
	26											
6	27											
	28											
	29											
7	30											

Simple and Practical Taxation

Exercise 8 (Page 82)

Month no	Week no	Pay in the week or month including Statutory Sick Pay/Statutory Maternity Pay (2) £	Total pay to date (3) £	Total free pay to date (Table A) (4a) £	K codes only — Total 'additional pay' to date (Table A) (4b) £	Total taxable pay to date i.e. column 3 minus column 4a or column 3 plus column 4b (5) £	Total tax due to date as shown by Taxable Pay Tables (6) £	K codes only — Tax due at end of current period Mark refunds 'R' (6a) £	K codes only — Regulatory limit i.e. 50% of column 2 entry (6b) £	Tax deducted or refunded in the week or month. Mark refunds 'R' (7) £	K codes only — Tax not deducted owing to the Regulatory limit (8) £	For employer's use
1	1											
	2											
	3											
	4	1100 00	1100 00		355 75	1455 75	323 89	323 89	550 00	323 89		
	5											
	6											
	7											
2	8	1200 00	2300 00		711 50	3011 50	671 02	347 13	600 00	347 13		
	9											
	10											
	11											
	12											
3	13	1400 00	3700 00		1067 25	4767 25	1064 16	393 14	700 00	393 14		
	14											
	15											
	16											
4	17	1250 00	4950 00		1423 00	6373 00	1422 78	358 62	625 00	358 62		
	18											
	19											
	20											
5	21	1500 00	6450 00		1778 75	8228 75	1838 68	415 90	750 00	415 90		
	22											
	23											
	24											
	25											
6	26											
	27											
	28											
	29											
7	30											

Exercise 9 (Page 91)

Employee	Average Weekly Earnings £	No of Qualifying Days in Week	Days Sick	SSP Payable in Week £
Jan	220	6	Sunday to Friday	£28.85
Joe	199	5	Sunday to Sunday	£23.08
Stuart	56	5	Tuesday to Friday	Nil
Donna	136	4	Monday to Wednesday	Nil

Exercise 10   (Page 97)   See next page

Exercise 11   (Page 101)

	£
Car Benefit £11,250 x 35%	3937
Less Discount for high mileage 2/3	(2625)
	1312
Less Discount for age 1/3	(437)
	875
Add Fuel Benefit	1280
Total Benefit	2155

Tax payable £2,155 @ 10% = £215.50

Exercise 10 (Page 97)

Earnings recorded in column 1a should not exceed the Upper Earnings Limit

For employer's use	Earnings on which employee's contributions payable *Whole pounds only* 1a £	Total of employee's and employer's contributions payable 1b £	Employee's contributions payable 1c £	Earnings on which employee's contributions at contracted-out rate payable included in col 1a *Whole pounds only* 1d £	Employee's contributions at contracted-out rate included in column 1c 1e £	Statutory Sick Pay in the week or month included in column 2 1f £	Statutory Maternity Pay in the week or month included in column 2 1g £	Statutory Maternity Pay recovered 1h £	Month no	Week no
										1
										2
										3
	1100	197 76	87 76						1	4
										5
										6
										7
	1200	217 76	97 76						2	8
										9
										10
										11
										12
	1400	257 76	117 76						3	13
										14
										15
										16
	1250	228 16	102 96						4	17
										18
										19
										20
	1500	277 76	127 76						5	21
										22
										23
										24
										25
									6	26
										27
										28
										29
									7	30
	Total c/fwd	Total c/fwd	Total c/fwd	Total c/fwd	Total c/fwd	Total c/fwd	Total c/fwd	Total c/fwd		

Exercise 12   (Page 106)

Susan's Class 4 liability:

	£
Net profit	29000
Upper limit for Class 4	25220
Less lower limit for Class 4	7310
Amount of profit liable	17910
Liability £17,910 x 6% =	£1,074.60

Exercise 13   (Page 117)

Total period of accounts 1 January 1997 to 31 December 1997 = 365 days

Financial Year 1996 = 1 January – 31 March 1997   = 90 days
Financial Year 1997 = 1 April 1997 – 31 December 1997 = 275 days

Financial Year 1996 = £124,000 x 90/365   = £30,575
Financial Year 1997 = £124,000 x 275/365   = £93,425
                                        Total   = £124,000

Corporation Tax due:

Financial Year 1996 = £30,575 x 24%   = £7,338.00
Financial Year 1997 = £93,425 x 21%   = £19,619.25
Total Corporation Tax Due   = £26,957.25

Exercise 14   (Page 123)

1)   £187 x ¼ = £46.75, payable 14/4/98

2)   £246 x ¼ = £61.50, payable 14/10/98

3)   £292 x ¼ = £73.00, payable 14/12/98

Did you remember that the dividend paid on 31/10/98 would have to be paid two weeks after the companies year end date of 30/11/98?

Answer to Jean's Car Example   (Page 172)

	£
Year 3 written down value b/fwd	6750
Writing down allowance (WDA) @ 25%	1688
New written down value (WDV)	5062

	£
Year 4 written down value b/fwd	5062
Writing down allowance (WDA) @ 25%	1266
New written down value (WDV)	3796

Continued

Answer to Marian's Car Example (Page 173)

	£
Year 2 written down value b/fwd	13000
Writing down allowance @ 25%	3000 x 70% = £2100 claim
New written down value	10000

	£
Year 3 written down value b/fwd	10000
Writing down allowance @ 25%	2500 x 70% = £1750 claim
New written down value	7500

Miscellaneous Tax Points

Miscellaneous Point 1 – Capital Allowances

Pat has a car which is used solely for business purposes and cost £12,000. She wants to agree the capital allowances with the tax inspector.

Cost of car	£12000
Writing down allowance (WDA) @ 25%	3000
Written down value (WDV)	9000

Pat can now claim a capital allowance of £3,000 against her taxable profit. However, if there is any private use of the vehicle, this must be reflected in the claim.

Consider the case of Jean who also has a car costing £12,000. However, she uses the vehicle 70% for business and 30% for private use.

Cost of car	£12000
Writing down allowance (WDA) @ 25%	3000 @ 70% = £2100
Written down value (WDV)	9000

Jean can only claim £2,100 against her profits; however, the asset value must be reduced by the full 25%. The remaining 'written down value' is then carried forward to the next year as follows:

Written down value b/fwd	£9000
Writing down allowance (WDA) @ 25%	2250
Written down value (WDV)	6750

Remember that, once again, the written down allowance will have to be reduced for any private use of the vehicle in that year. Complete the capital allowance calculation for Jean's car for years 3 and 4, ignoring any private use adjustments.

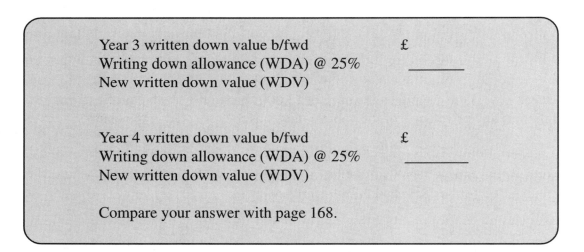

Year 3 written down value b/fwd   £ _____
Writing down allowance (WDA) @ 25%   _____
New written down value (WDV)

Year 4 written down value b/fwd   £ _____
Writing down allowance (WDA) @ 25%   _____
New written down value (WDV)

Compare your answer with page 168.

Cars costing over £12,000

Cars costing over £12,000 are restricted to a maximum claim of £12,000 x 25% = £3,000 for capital allowance purposes. Consider the following example, again using a restriction of 30% for private use.

Marian purchases a car costing £16,000

Cost of car	£16000.00	
Writing down allow @ 25% of £12000	3000.00	x 70% = £2100 claim
Written down value	13000.00	

In the above example, only £2,100 (£3,000 less private use of £900) can be claimed against profit. Continue the computation for the following two years. Note that, in year 3, the WDA is below £12,000 so no value limit applies.

Year 2 written down value b/fwd £
Writing down allowance @ 25% _____ x 70% = £   claim
New written down value

Year 3 written down value b/fwd £
Writing down allowance @ 25% _____ x 70% = £   claim
New written down value

Compare your answer with page 169.

A more comprehensive example follows showing additions and disposals for a business with plant and motor vehicles.

Bert, a sole trader, has the following information for his accounting period ended 30.4.96.

	£
Written down value of pool at 1.5.95	16000
Motor car purchased – 10% private use	15000
Plant purchased	25000
Plant disposed of	8000

		Pooled Plant £	Motor Car £
Written down value b/fwd		16000	
Additions:	Motor car		15000
	Plant	25000	_____
		41000	15000
Less disposals		(8000)	_____
		33000	15000
Writing down allowance @ 25%		(8250)	(3000) (less private use £300)
New written down value (WDV)		24750	12000

In the above example, we have taken account of additions and disposals to an existing pool of plant in order to demonstrate how this is computed. The claim in respect of the motor vehicle is restricted to the maximum value of £12,000. Remember, separate pools must be created for

- all motor vehicles costing less than £12,000
- each car costing more than £12,000
- each asset used partly for private use.

Capital allowances are only available to owners of an asset. Ownership is extended to cover assets purchased under a hire purchase agreement. However, if the asset is being leased or rented, capital allowances are not available because the business does not actually own the asset. Instead, the business claims an allowance for the leasing or rental costs actually incurred. Capital allowances for the commencement or cessation of a business are complicated. For those who need to know, a more detailed explanation follows.

Miscellaneous Point 2 – Opening Years Assessment Rules Under New Provisions

First accounts for short period ending in tax year of commencement

Where the first accounting period is a short one which ends in the same tax year in which the business commenced, it is necessary to prepare a second set of accounts before you would be able to compute the first year's tax assessment. This is because it is based on the period from commencement to the following 5th April.

The second year profits would then be determined by reference to the first full twelve month accounting period to the normal accounting date.

Any overlap profits would be calculated using the second full year's accounts. Let's look at an example of this.

Wendie commenced trading on 1 July 1995 making up her accounts to 31 December 1995 and annually to 31 December thereafter.

Wendie's adjusted profits are:

6 months to 31.12.95	£12,000
Year ended 31.12.96	£29,200
Year ended 31.12.97	£32,000

The assessable profits are:

1995/96	1.7.95 – 31.12.95	£12,000
	Plus 1.1.96 – 5.4.96 (95/365 x £29,200)	£7,600
		£19,600
1996/97 Year ended 31.12.96		£29,200
1997/98 Year ended 31.12.97		£32,000

Overlap profits would be those between 1.1.95 – 5.4.96 = £7,600

First accounts for more than 12 months ending in second tax year of assessment

Where the first accounts are prepared for a period that is longer than 12 months and ends in the second year of assessment, then the period to be taken into account for the second tax year is the 12 months ending with the chosen accounting date. Let us look at an example of this.

Keith commenced trading on 1 July 1995 and makes up accounts to 31 October 1996 and annually to 31 October thereafter.

Keith's adjusted profits are:

16 Months to 31.10.96	£33,000
12 Months to 31.10.97	£22,000

The assessable profits are:

1995/96	1.7.95 – 5.4.96 (279/488 x £33,000)	£18,866
1996/97	1.11.95 – 31.10.96 (365/488 x £33,000)	£24,682
1997/98	Year ended 31.10.97	£22,000

Overlap profits will be £18,866 + £24,682 - £33,000 = £10,548
as this is the amount of doubly taxed profit.

There are also special rules for the assessment of profit in the circumstances where:

(i)   The first year accounts end in the third tax year of assessment, *and*

(ii)   The first set of accounts are for less than a 12 month period but end in the second tax year of assessment.

We will not cover these in detail in this book and you should take advice if these circumstances apply to your business.

The Old Taxation System

These rules relate to businesses which were already in operation on 5 April 1994. These businesses are taxed under the 'preceding year basis'. This means that the business is taxed during the *current* tax year on profits earned in the *previous* tax year. The example below is for the tax year 1995/96. The diagram shows a business with an accounting year end date of 28 February 1995.

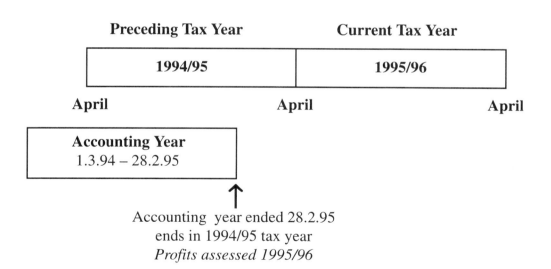

The tax would be paid in two equal instalments. These would be in January and July 1996.

This system produces all sorts of peculiarities, especially during the opening and closing years of a business. Therefore, the new system has been designed which should be easier to understand for the self employed.

Transitional Arrangements Between 'Old' and 'New' Systems

Eventually, every business will be taxed on the current year basis. This, of course, is not a problem for businesses which commenced trading after 5 April 1994. These businesses are taxed on a current year basis from the outset. However, businesses which commenced trading before 5 April 1994 will need to be changed over to the new (ie current year) basis of taxation.

How will businesses switch from the existing 'preceding year basis' to the 'current year basis'? The answer is that the Inland Revenue has announced that the 1996/97 tax year will be a transitional year. The profit assessed in 1996/97 will be a percentage of the combined profits of two accounting periods. These periods are:

Period 1 The profits of the accounting year which ends in the 1996/97 tax year

Period 2 The profits which would have been taxed in 1996/97 under the old 'preceding year' rules.

For example, for a business with a 30 April accounting date, Period 1 would be the profits for the year ended 30 April 1996. Period 2 would be the profit for the year ended 30 April 1995, ie the accounting year ends in the 1995/96 tax year and jumps one year to 1996/97 under the preceding year's rules.

At first glance, it may seem that the business will have to pay tax on *two* years' profits. However, only a percentage of the combined profit is assessed for tax. Normally, this percentage will be 50%. To be precise, the Inland Revenue will add together the total days in both accounting periods and divide by 365 to arrive at the assessable percentage of profit for 1996/97. Confused? Let's look at an example.

Example

A business prepares its accounts regularly to 30 April each year. The profits for each accounting year are as follows:

Accounts Year	Profits
Y/ended 30.4.95	£22,000
Y/ended 30.4.96	£24,000
Total profits earned	**£46,000**

These profits will, under the transitional provisions, be assessed as follows:

1996/97	Y/ended 30.4.95	£22,000
	Y/ended 30.4.96	£24,000
365 days/731* days x 46,000		£22,967
Total profits assessed 1996/97		**£22,967**

We can see, therefore, that the major benefit from the transitional rules is that part of the profits of the business occurring in the transitional period will not be assessed!

In the example, the position is as follows:

Total profits earned as above	£46,000
Less Total profits assessed	£22,967
Total profits unassessed	**£23,033**

The percentage of profits unassessed may increase if the accounting date is changed and the transitional period becomes longer. Professional advice should be sought regarding such a change.

* There are 731 days in the transitional period as 1996 is a leap year.

For existing businesses, where their accounting period will straddle the tax year ended 5 April 1997, there will also be a period of overlap profits. This period of overlap profits will run from the commencement of their accounting period prior to 5 April 1997 and run to 5 April 1997.

Using the above example, let us look at a diagram showing the transitional period and the period of overlap.

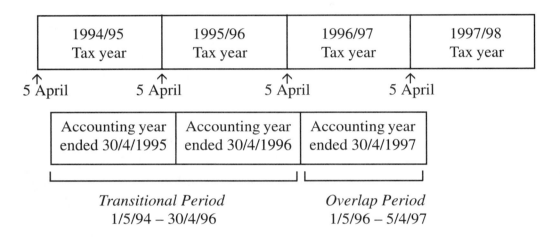

We can see from the diagram the period to be taken into account for overlap profits would be the period from 1 May 1996 to 5 April 1997. This is because the accounting year ended 30 April 1997 will form the assessable profit under the current year basis for the 1997/98 tax year whereas 11/12ths of the profits (the period between 1 May 1996 and 5 April 1997) have been earned during the 1996/97 tax year. Again, the same provisions apply for granting overlap profits, ie the earlier of a change in accounting date resulting in an accounting period of more than 12 months or at the cessation of the trade. Because overlap profits are eroded by inflation, it may be better to change the accounting date of the business to a period of more than 12 months. However, advice must be taken as there are special rules relating to a change of accounting date.

Index

Through Kogan Page all readers can enjoy the benefits of Call Sciences' *Personal Assistant*® - the complete Call Management System

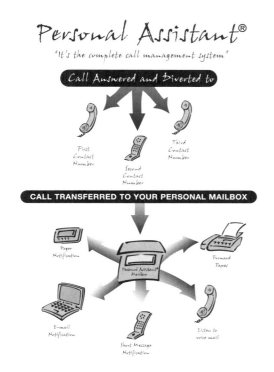

CALL ME – Your clients, friends and family only need ONE NUMBER to contact you rather than separate numbers for mobile, home, office and fax.

FAX ME – You choose where and when your faxes are delivered to any fax machine – you control whether your faxes are forwarded straight away or stored until you collect them.

FIND ME – *Personal Asistant*® searches you at up to 3 locations according to your typical weekly availability schedule – and it even remembers where it last found you.

When you are not available, your calls are automatically routed to voice mail. Whenever a message is received, you are notified by pager, GSM short message or e-mail.

Why have a *Personal Assistant*® number?

- Your own receptionist 24 hours a day
- Your personal number is never engaged
- Greets your callers in a professional manner
- Holds your contact numbers and knows where to find you
- Tells you who is calling before putting them through
- Transfers to another number or voice mail part way through a call
- Knows when you do not normally wish to be disturbed
- Takes voice and fax messages when you are not available
- Faxes delivered to any fax machine
- Charge card option for outgoing calls

All for less than 25p per day

Call Sciences™

QMS
ISO 9002
REGISTERED FIRM

Call 0800 689 9999 today to activate your Personal Assistant®!

Sage & Vector Books

What **PROFIT** am I making?

How much **VAT** do I owe?

Is my **INVOICING** up to date?

Who is over their **CREDIT LIMIT**?

How much **CASH** do I owe?

Sage Instant Accounting

If you're responsible for running a business or looking after the books, finding the right answers to financial questions can seem like a full time job itself. The solution is Sage Instant Accounting.

Sage Instant Accounting is quite simply the easiest way to take care of your accounting needs. With the touch of a button you can access all the information you need concerning your business finances, without tedious and time consuming paperwork.

It's easy to use, because it has a built in demonstration and start-up user guide (commonly called a "wizard"!) that helps you every step of the way, plus 30 days free telephone support from our experts.

From invoicing to credit limits, from chasing payments to sales figures, from VAT to forecasting, Instant Accounting has the answer. No wonder most accountants in practice recommend Sage to their clients.

Sage Instant Payroll

Sage Instant Payroll is the easiest way to manage your payroll for up to 10 employees, saving you time and money - and keeping you fully in control of this important function.

At the touch of a button, it calculates pay and prints out payslips, greatly speeding up this crucial task. What used to take hours with now take you minutes. It has a full on-line library of help so it's very easy to use.

About Sage

Sage are the world's leading supplier of accounting and payroll software with over a million users world-wide. Sage have over 250,000 users in the UK alone from businesses of all shapes and sizes and every industry category. All Sage products are easily upgradeable, so your Sage solution can expand along with your business.

Sage Vector Books **Special Offer**

Putting yourself firmly in control of your company won't break the bank. In fact, Sage Instant Accounting and Instant Payroll are great value for money at just £99 each.

And if you buy both now, Sage and Vector books have agreed a **special discount offer of £169**, that's a saving of over £30.

To order Instant Accounting, Instant Payroll, or both, simply call the number below or fax back this order form to Sage. Or find us on the Internet at www.sage.com

Fax: 0191 255 0304

Alternatively **telephone** us on
0800 44 77 77 `Ext 590`

I want to make my business more efficient - in an instant

☐ Please send me Sage Instant Accounting at £99 (inc VAT)

☐ Please send me Sage Payroll at £99 (inc VAT)

☐ Please send me Sage Instant Accounting and Payroll at the special price of £169 (inc VAT)

☐ Please send me more information on Sage Instant Accounting and Payroll

Please add £4.70 for postage and packing.

☐ Please invoice my company

☐ I enclose a cheque payable to The Sage Group plc

☐ Please charge my Credit Card
MasterCard/Visa No:

Title: (Mr, Mrs, Miss, Ms) _____ Initial: _____ Surname: _____

Job Title: _____ Company: _____

Address: _____

Postcode: _____

Expiry date:

Signature:

Tel: _____ Fax: _____